On Time!
On Task!
On a Mission!

On Time!
On Task!
On a Mission!

A Year in the Life of a Middle School Principal

Christopher M. Spence

Fernwood Publishing • Halifax

Editing: Anne Webb
Cover photo: Richard Pierre
Photos: Zelia Tavares and Paul Burton
Design and production: Larissa Holman and Beverley Rach
Printed and bound in Canada by: Hignell Printing Limited

A publication of:
Fernwood Publishing
Site 2A, Box 5
Black Point, Nova Scotia
B0J 1B0

Fernwood Publishing Company Limited gratefully acknowledges the financial support of the Department of Canadian Heritage, the Nova Scotia Department of Tourism and Culture and the Canada Council for the Arts for our publishing program.

NOVA SCOTIA
Tourism and Culture

Le Conseil des Arts du Canada | The Canada Council for the Arts

"Believe You Can" by Margo Pfeiff. Copyright © 2001 by the Reader's Digest Magazines Limited. Reprinted by permission from the June 2001 issue of Reader's Digest.
"Game plan" by Kristin Rushowy. Copyright © 1999 Toronto Star. Reprinted with permission—The Toronto Star Syndicate.

National Library of Canada Cataloguing in Publication

Spence, Christopher Michael, 1962-
On time! On task! On a mission!: a year in the life of a middle school principal / Christopher Spence.

Includes bibliographical references.
ISBN 1-55266-094-X

1. Lawrence Heights Middle School. 2. School improvement programs—Case studies. 3. School improvement programs—Ontario—Toronto. 4. Urban schools—Case studies. 5. Spence, Christopher Michael, 1962- I. Title.

LA2325.S65A3 2002   373.12'07   C2002-903643-7

Contents

Acknowledgements

One of the wonderful things about working at Lawrence Heights Middle School is that I have met so many extraordinary people and have had the privilege of working with them. Expressing my gratitude is my ultimate pleasure. This book is dedicated to the Lawrence Heights students, staff and community.

Thank you—your encouragement, acceptance, support, trust and honesty brought out all I have to offer. I could not have asked for a better experience.

Thank you to the most thoughtful, capable, dedicated, knowledgeable and hardworking staff that any principal ever had the privilege of enjoying.

Thank you to the most enthusiastic, talented, spirited and intelligent student body anywhere and to a community rich in diversity, thought and energy.

All of you have been my inspiration and superb guides. You made our journey to excellence at Lawrence Heights remarkable.

Thanks go to our trustee, Sheine Mankosvky, and our superintendent, Karen Forbes, for their support and commitment to making a difference.

To my publisher Errol Sharpe, and the rest of the Fernwood team, I convey my deepest thanks for their unwavering commitment to a project whose potential value they saw from the beginning. A special thanks for the brilliant work of my editor, Anne Webb, for bringing it all together.

And once again I thank my family, who remind me that I did not get here on my own. They sacrifice for me, support me and pray for me. Thanks to my parents Sydney and Enez Spence, my wife Marcia, my brother Everard and sister Jacqueline who taught me the value of an education and that learning never stops. They taught me to never lose sight of my dreams and goals, and to always believe in myself. They taught me that to stand up for what I believe is just and right, no matter the cost. They have always been behind me, loving and supporting me, no matter how crazy they viewed my various escapades. Most of all, they accept and believe in me. I would not be who I am today without them. May this book stand as a testimony to my admiration and love for you all.

To the children in my life

*Briana, Jacob, Chandra, Taylor, Isabelle, Ann, Ruby
and the children of the Lawrence Heights community*

Introduction

Inspiring Hope

As an educator my attention has been captured by the plight of increasing numbers of children and youth who are in circumstances that place them at risk of educational failure, particularly in inner-city communities. The quality of life in these communities is jeopardized by poverty, lack of employment opportunities, poor health care, crime, fragmented services and despair—but this is only one side of the story. The other side of the story is that there are schools like Lawrence Heights which are rich in culture, energy, talent and other resources that promote excellence in learning. These resources can further the capacity of individuals to overcome adversity and develop the ability to persevere in school in spite of their circumstances.

Influences such as teachers' actions and expectations, effective instruction and curriculum, schoolwide policies and school climate play key roles in improving student learning, motivation and attitudes toward school. The staff at Lawrence Heights believe there should be no excuses, only improvements. Whatever our disagreements about education may be, there is one expectation we all share; education should improve one's chances of leading a good life.

In 1746 French philosopher Denis Diderot said, "only passions, great passions, can elevate the soul to great things. I have a passion for the work we do and those I lead." I am enormously proud to be an educator. It is this passion for my work and for pursuing student achievement that has inspired me to write this book. This book was written during the 1999–2000 school year at Lawrence Heights Middle School.

Navigating the turbulent waters of educational change takes passion, purpose and vision. It takes people who place the interests of students before all others and who work with other staff to promote workable solutions. The staff at Lawrence Heights are willing to provide the level of commitment, dedication and energy needed to keep the students on the road to success.

As the principal of Lawrence Heights my approach is simple: put together the best people, support them and give them every opportunity to do their best work. The best way to do this is equally simple: put together programs and policies that create a culture of excellence. That ideal culture has been a determinant part of the way we do business.

As we undertake our journey to excellence, a number of values inform and guide our reactions to people and events. We place the interests of our children first and foremost; above all, regardless of cost and personal inconvenience, we maintain absolute integrity in the performance of our duties, insisting on excellence and diligence from ourselves and our students with no exceptions or excuses. This is understood to mean that we have high expectations and superior standards for everyone; we permit individuals to grow professionally, promoting a system of accountability that gives staff the tools they need to be successful in their efforts with their students.

Over the course of my teaching career, my mentors have always emphasized the importance of documenting. I can effectively plan and learn from thinking critically, analyzing, questioning and discussing my daily experiences, thoughts, actions and ideas by jotting them down. Chapters three to five are exerpts from my day-to-day documentation. As a principal I have tried to make documentation a part of the school's organizational culture and have made daybooks mandatory and in some instances a part of staff performance objectives. Getting started on the road to meaningful documentation may seem to be overwhelming, but it only hurts the first time. Once you have gotten over the initial hurdle and have established a regular routine, it becomes easy.

This book was hard to write. It was hard to live through not knowing at times whether we were doing the right thing at Lawrence Heights. The book may initially seem discouraging, but ultimately I hope readers will see the resilient and transcendent qualities of the students and efforts of the staff. This book is not about social despair, but about hope.

Hope is what drives improvement. Improving schools and, ultimately, our students' performance is the best hope for the future. To make the necessary changes, we have to re-build the foundations of our educational system. We need to start by inspiring hope such that our students believe they will get the education they need to succeed; our teachers find they are supported in the classroom and recognized for their performance; and parents find that they can be involved in a system that will prepare their children for the future.

In my professional experience every child I have ever seen in kindergarten came to school enthusiastic and willing to learn. They absorb knowledge like a sponge, but for far too many something goes wrong. For each additional year these children stay in school, they fall further behind, not because they cannot learn, but because the system somehow failed to prepare them to learn. How is it that in a few short years children diminish in thought, behaviour, acceptance, self-esteem, test scores and interpersonal skills? How does this happen?

In my research for this book, I visited middle schools and elementary schools. As I looked across the schoolyards, I saw the innocent faces of children filled with hope and a desire to learn. They had little understanding of what their futures would be. At the same time, many students and schools are succeeding. On a visit to our feeder schools, I saw once again the stimulating and challenging environments that the principals, the staff and the community have created for the students. They write grant proposals and have fundraising events to get money for computers, supplies and nutrition programs, all in an effort to meet the needs of their students.

Schools as a Unit of Change

The staff at Lawrence Heights are becoming increasingly aware that it is no longer enough to educate some of our children. Our society is changing, our demographics are changing, and so too, must our educational beliefs and practice change. The prime purpose of education is the development of the human intellect in all its dimensions (social, cultural, moral, emotional and physical). Education is the means by which a nation prepares those who will work to sustain it. Therefore schools have a role, along with parents, other social agencies and the wider community, in shaping values, attitudes and responsible behaviours. But they must not and cannot be expected to meet this challenge alone.

Creating schools that bring out the best in each and every child is what we as parents, teachers, administrators and members of the community want. We want to ensure that an educational foundation is in place to provide all children the opportunity to acquire the skills, values and knowledge they need to be productive, responsible members of society. However, we are faced with competing and sometimes conflicting needs. We encourage and teach our children to preserve what we value of our past, to respond to the demands of the present, and to be well prepared for the future.

What we are seeing in Ontario is a well intentioned but conceptually shallow effort to improve our schools. The current effort to improve the quality and standards of education through testing is no novelty, evidence being the 1994 Royal Commission On Learning. We have been there before. Successful efforts at school reform entail a substantially deeper analysis of schools and their relationships to communities and teachers than has thus far been undertaken in Ontario.

If the larger society and the government talk only about tests and standards and do not talk about the ways that teachers, principals, students and communities can work together to improve student achievement, nothing is going to happen. Our change efforts need to go beyond the school if we are going to make significant improvements to what goes on within it.

Thus far our change priorities fail to develop what Daniel Goleman

(1997) calls the "emotional intelligence" of students and teachers. Emotional intelligence is the capacity to create positive outcomes in our relationships with others and ourselves. Educating for emotional intelligence is not just for students anymore. School leaders must also develop the social competencies needed to achieve complex goals. The most critical competencies required for effective leadership include self-awareness and self-control, motivation and persistence, empathy and the ability to form mutually satisfying relationships (see Table 1). As educational leaders we can cultivate these vital traits through well designed training programs that actually add value to students' classroom learning and teachers' professional learning.

Administrators are individuals who make decisions about the amount of support change efforts receive. The amount of support we give to innovations and opportunities for our leaders can be the reason for their success or failure. Given this influential role, we must have an understanding of the change

Table 1: The Five Components of Emotional Intelligence at Work

	Definition	Hallmarks
Self Awareness	-the ability to recognize and understand your moods, emotions and drives, as well as their effects on others	-self confidence -realistic self-assessment -self-deprecating sense of humour
Self Regulation	-the ability to control or redirect disruptive impulses and moods -the propensity to suspend judgement—to think before acting	-trustworthiness, integrity -comfort with ambiguity -openness to change
Motivation	-a passion to work for reasons that go beyond money or status -a propensity to pursue goals with energy and persistence	-strong drive to achieve -optimism, even in the face of failure -organizational committment
Empathy	-the ability to understand the emotional make-up of other people -skill in treating people according to their emotional reactions	-expertise in building and retaining talent -cross cultural sensitivity -service to clients and customers
Social Skill	-proficiency in managing relationships and building networks -an ability to find common ground and build support	-effectiveness in leading change -persuasiveness -expertise in building and leading teams

Source: Goleman 1997

process and its implications. Michael Fullan, a recognized authority on the subject of educational change, contends that change is a process and not an event, and that the school is still the unit of change. This suggests that while the school is the central and primary focus, it is surrounded by outside forces that have an impact on the school.

One such outside force is competition. As parents are given more choices for their children's education, schools are facing this factor usually associated with the business world. It seems that in order to survive, schools must adopt a market driven philosophy that requires them to see students, parents and the community, and anyone else who comes into contact with the school, as customers. Successful businesses know that appropriate attitudes, behaviour and communication are integral to providing good customer service.

To gain control over the school's environment we must change our stance towards it. Fullan and Hargreaves (1998) cite several reasons why schools need to connect more effectively with the wider world beyond them:

- Schools cannot shut their gates and leave the outside world on the doorstep.
- More diversity demands greater flexibility.
- The technology juggernaut is breaking down the walls of schooling.
- Schools are one of the last hopes for rescuing and reinventing community.
- Teachers can do with more help and so can parents and communities.
- Education is essential for democracy.
- Market competition, parental choice and individual self-management are redefining how schools relate to their wider environments.
- Schools can no longer be indifferent to what kinds of living and working await their students when they move into the adult world.
- The pressures of today's complex environments are relentless, and contradictory; and our existing structures are exhausted. (Fullan and Hargreaves 1998: 6)

As our schools become more and more permeable, we need to consider how to connect our internal struggles with the wider community and how to bring the community into the school to pursue our various struggles with us. To effectively facilitate this process we must also go deeper into the heart of teaching to rediscover the passion and purpose that makes teaching and learning exciting.

The book, *What's Worth Fighting For Out There?* (Fullan and Hargreaves 1998) is a must read for all educators involved in change processes. It devotes full chapters to guidelines for action for teachers, principals and governments. It is filled with insights that will help school educators take responsibility for reform. I have used the book as a compass in my leadership development and strongly recommend it to the Lawrence Heights staff.

Fullan and Hargreaves talk about how teachers can work together for positive change, how they can collaborate with others outside the classroom to improve what goes on within it, and how principals can support their teachers to make this happen. They offer six guidelines to further help educational leaders achieve success.

> First, respect those you want to silence—learn from your opponents and mobilize people to tackle tough problems. Second, move toward the danger in forming new alliances—work with, rather than against, such external factors as the community and policy makers. Third, manage emotionally as well as rationally—pay attention to emotional health and put a high priority on re-culturing, as well as restructuring. Fourth, fight for lost causes—understand the power of hope as a resource for strength and change. Fifth, steer clear of false certainty, and sixth base risk on security. (Fullan and Hargreaves 1998: 10)

They leave the reader with a clear message about responsibilities and actions that should be taken and supported by educators.

Chapter 1

Hope Drives Improvement

I was drawn to the teaching profession because I enjoy working with young people. I see teaching as a constant challenge. A teacher introduces children to new worlds of information. True educators must help their pupils develop the intellectual capacity for self-awareness, and those who teach learn as well.

The role of the school has changed dramatically over the years. The traditionalist approach was based on strict discipline and the mastering of school subjects; any thought given to the child was in relation to their progress in these subjects. Times have changed, thanks partially to Friedrich Froebel, the founder of kindergarten. Froebel's vision was to stimulate an appreciation and love for children and to provide them with a new, but small world in which they could play with their own age group and experience their first gentle taste of independence. The Froebelian movement (1870–1945) stands for the child centred school and for growth. Froebelian educators are interested in the emotional development of the child, their interests and attitudes—they are interested in the development of the whole child.

Educators have become more concerned with the kind of person they are helping to produce, ideally anyway, and with the definition of the verb to educate—which means to give intellectual and moral training. Educators are now helping learners become decision makers and critical thinkers by making them feel they can contribute their ideas and make a difference.

As a teacher I have always wanted to do the utmost to enhance the joy of learning. To see students step into each new challenge able to communicate, cooperate and show consideration is a tremendous and gratifying experience. Knowing that the children will gain practical and useful knowledge from these abilities later in life only heightens that sense of gratification.

My First Teaching Assignment

I entered teaching hoping to change the world, or at least the little bit of it that I touched. And so I volunteered to teach in a special needs school in spite of the cautionary tales from friends and colleagues.

"You're going to teach in that neighbourhood?"

"Are you crazy?"

"Well, just do your time and get out."

Special needs schools are determined by the average and median income of families with school-aged children, parental education, proportion of lone parent families, recent immigration, housing type and student mobility. The perception of the severity of conditions such as poverty, racism and violence in special needs schools had led many in my teachers' college graduating class to wonder whether anything would really help. Though few schools are immune to the problems that affect inner-city classrooms, social and economic distress compound the difficulties. When educators address socio-economic difficulties in the community and in schools, we also face ideological issues including the false notion that students in these communities cannot attain the same academic and social goals as more economically privileged children.

I have always believed in the importance of our educational system having the ability to educate those who attend special needs schools. If education is truly going to be a means of social mobility and a liberating experience then schools need to provide students with the opportunity to achieve those ends. Many of our students will not move out of their community; we will be providing the same opportunities to their children. In a special needs school equal funding may not be adequate funding, because these schools may require an initial extra investment just to be elevated to an acceptable baseline for academic achievement.

I knew I was going to make a difference the day I walked into the school of my first teaching assignment. The principal did not make many promises but she did offer to provide unconditional support. I found that was all I needed. I researched the school and the principal, as that was one of the messages taught to us at teachers' college. The volumes of testimonials from teachers about their principal's dynamic and motivating style, her ability to communicate and her genuine concern for the individual student and teacher made it a perfect fit.

On the first day of classes students and staff were asked to congregate in the cafeteria to pick up their timetables, classroom assignment and list of students. Every teacher had a sign with her or his name on it and students had to check the lists and then move to where their teacher was. I sat patiently not really knowing how the students would react to me. After all I was a first year teacher and had heard horror stories about how new teachers were treated. In a few short moments a group of five Black boys approached me and one of them asked:

"Are you Mr. Spence?"

The others looked on with anticipation waiting for my response. "Yes," I replied. "I am Mr. Sp...." Before I could even finish the sentence they were gone. They came back two minutes later and this time there were almost ten of them gazing at me.

"Are you sure you're Mr. Spence?"

"Yes," I replied. Well, what took place after that is something that I will never forget. The group of students began to celebrate.

"I told you, I told you ... he is Black and he is our teacher."

"Yes, yes, yes ... " they went on.

Nothing could have prepared me for what I was about to face in the classroom. Students routinely came to school without a pen or pencil or anything on which to write. Some students had come to believe that simply attending school every day and taking up space at a desk was all they needed to do. There were students who could hardly write their names, read a simple paragraph, or answer a simple math problem. Some students cared nothing about their education. Not all students could be described as such, but there were more examples of uninterested than there were ideal students well on their way to academic success.

I was basically teaching elementary school to middle school students. I, like most of my colleagues, worked my brains out to move my students up a grade level or two by the end of the year. At the time, I was angry at the system for being so dysfunctional and for failing so many of my students. I even boldly stated this to our superintendent who had casually asked how things were going. He did listen and was as concerned as I was about what seemed to be insoluble problems.

The fact that these students were so academically behind never sat well with me or with a number of other staff members. Our response to this was to have school on Saturdays, during vacations, and at night to make up the difference—whatever it takes. I never made peace with the fact that these kids were almost out of the race of life at such an early age because they lacked education. I resented that many of our students moving on to high school the following year were not prepared. The high school teachers were going to look at the dismal level of academic achievement of their classes and blame us middle school teachers as incompetent, in exactly the same way as we often viewed the elementary teachers.

I also discovered that middle school students who cannot read or write almost always decide that the time and energy it would take to learn is not worth the effort. I found that if a student cannot read, it is nearly impossible to teach her or him how to write.

I was young and idealistic, had neither family nor serious commitments of my own and would have been willing to do anything to get my students caught up to grade level. Fortunately, I have had great principals that have allowed me to dream a little and to hold onto some of those ideals. Now there were the naysayers who questioned, "If they can't get the material in five days what makes you think they will get it in six?" Some teachers continued to make reference to the background of the students and viewed them through the deficit model—they are coming from disadvantaged backgrounds, single parent families and therefore have deficits. Some of these teachers had come to regard the situation as normal. They had made their peace with the fact that these students were never going to catch up. I never had much time for those teachers.

At all three special needs schools where I have worked there have been some exceptional leaders and teachers seemingly born into the role. They were so gifted and talented that I could not imagine them doing anything else as valuable or as satisfying; their lives revolved around the school and their students. These advocates and educators demonstrated that rare ability to adjust their teaching style to the individual. They always had the highest expectations for their students inside and outside of the classroom, but most importantly they cared. They just wanted the kids to succeed. In fact they seemed to want this more than the kids themselves. These same teachers are the cornerstones of any school. They are the ones who the kids love and respect.

But even the best laid plans for improvement prepared by myself, administrators and these teachers, many of whom were much more experienced than I was, always seemed to stall and have difficulty gaining momentum. We find, especially in special needs schools, that as educators we are called upon to do a lot more than teach. With the demise of the church, family and neighbourhood, teachers find they must also be willing to serve as guidance counsellors, social workers and surrogate parents. In this era of malice and greed, teaching requires a moral courage that is tragically unfashionable.

At Lawrence Heights teachers must expertly balance scholarship with high standards and deep caring. In my experience at special needs schools I have seen teachers buy meals for students who were hungry and attend court for those involved with the law. I have seen teachers stand in for uninterested parents, and give up their weekends and evenings to drive students to an event. I have seen teachers give out their phone numbers. I have seen teachers expect the most and strive to get the best from all their students.

The reality is that most parents in special needs communities work long hours just to pay the rent and put food on the table, and are not able to actively involve themselves in the education of their children or come to see their children's teachers. Through no fault of their own, they almost always leave the educating up to us. Many families live in apartments with little or no place in which to study or to do homework. Such households are so busy meeting their basic needs, that there is little time to read for pleasure.

Some of my student's parents hardly even checked their children's homework or report cards. Many parents looked at school as a place where their children would learn how to read, write and behave before going to work to help out their family economically. Some of my students at the middle school level already had more education than their parents—any kind of help with homework would have to come from an older brother or sister whose own education was often far from complete. Academically speaking, my students all too often were on their own.

University was an unknown quantity which, while prestigious and desirable in the abstract, seemed expensive and out of reach. The typical student in my class knew no one (besides their teachers) who had been to university.

I say all this not to make excuses for my students' underachievement, but to understand the circumstances they were coming from. Two of the most important factors influencing a child's achievement in the early years of schooling are socioeconomics and whether the child has been read to at home before beginning school and has seen her or his parents reading. I suspect this does not change too much in the later grades. Therefore, in order to know where students are going we have to know where they are coming from. It is then up to the school to take the necessary steps to ensure equity of outcome.

Too many of our students lacked academic discipline and they often appeared to have more pressing concerns on their mind. I, like many of my colleagues, wanted my students to arrive at school with their basic needs met so that they could devote one hundred percent of their attention to learning. More often than not I was frustrated in this endeavour. Many students appeared to have been conditioned to simply go through the motions of learning rather than to truly work hard and as a consequence truly learn.

I did have special classes and students who I will never forget. There were the students outstanding in every respect and who would do well wherever they found themselves; it was both a pleasure and a privilege to teach them. It was not uncommon for other staff and me to take them home for the weekend or out for an activity such as a game, a concert or a play. These students came to class every day ready to learn. They had a positive attitude, goals and dreams about what they wanted to do with their lives

Some students in the class wasted their time and mine and were highly immature in their approach to their future. Whatever their plans were, school played only a marginal role. But these students too could learn. Nothing was more satisfying than reaching one of these learners and uniquely touching them. This made one realize the power of education.

I particularly enjoyed teaching a sixth grade class in which all the students were boys. Most of them were Black and many of them did not have a positive Black or male role model in their lives. They were so used to getting Ds and Fs that they viewed school as little more than temporary incarceration that provided the opportunity to fraternize with friends. But what a year we had. We started with the lowest class average math test scores and ended with one of the highest (87 percent). Through hard work, high expectations and some loving, these youngsters proved they were capable students. I was really impressed with their commitment to learn. We came in on Saturdays and every single student would show up. We were on a mission and each and every class member bought into it. I still recall when I was doing a lesson and sensed that I was losing the students due to fatigue or what have you, I could literally say, "you know this stuff is kind of boring. Let's do something else," and they would all reply, "yea sounds good." Well, it did not matter if I said, "let's re-write the dictionary," they would have thought that was the greatest activity in the world. The rapport was so strong and so positive that the results were great.

One student named Robbie put high expectations on himself and was easily frustrated. He rarely took risks because he did not like to be wrong. Robbie used to become particularly withdrawn in math. He was identified as having a learning disability. He had great difficulty with basic arithmetic skills, ordering and grouping. I observed that Robbie had a huge baseball card collection. He was a sports fanatic. I figured if there was one way to get Robbie experimenting with numbers, it might be with his card collection.

On the back of baseball cards are the players' career statistics. I started out by asking Robbie to put his cards in groups according to position: "How many shortstops do you have? How many pitchers do you have? For what position do you have the most cards? In what position do you have the least?" Robbie was on task and definitely enjoyed doing this.

We then discussed what the numbers on the back of the cards meant. Robbie found this to be most interesting as he really had no idea, for example, how many strikeouts (SO) a player had, or how many doubles (2B) the player hit. I would ask him, "How many triples does this player have compared to another player? Does he have more or less? How many less? How many more?" We would do this for the various players. I would ask Robbie and he would ask me. Throughout the exercise, he was on task but more importantly he was discovering number sense.

There were other students in the class who also enjoyed collecting and trading baseball cards, so I decided to get these students in a group after school and we would ask each other questions, all the while playing with numbers. We did not call it math because that might have spoiled their fun.

This kind of magic was made possible by supportive administrators who gave me an opportunity that I will never forget. But more than anything I realized how important it was to have the highest of expectations for my students. I offered strict academic and disciplinary guidelines, involved parents (contracts and phone calls) and demonstrated that I cared for my students and their futures, as would any effective teacher. One of the things that I discovered was the need to know my students. I constantly asked myself, "who are my learners and what are their needs?" Reflecting on that question and observing my students always kept me focused and my purpose real.

Schools were never designed to be surrogate parents or counselling centres. They are supposed to teach people how to read, write and think. But without a little passion and caring for my students I am not going anywhere. That is personified in a special needs school, because for too many students and parents life was something that happened to them instead of something forged by themselves. Hardships were part of their destiny, and to endure rather than to change them was to succeed. I remember asking an "at-risk" student about his aspirations and moving out of the community. He was surprised by the question. "No. I have always lived here. I guess I will always live here. This is my home." The possibility of an alternative life simply had not occurred to him. What I came to feel with time was an immense sadness over this kind of revelation. For students to not even consider alternatives seemed so limiting.

Effective Schools

Much of my philosophy on education and schooling developed and evolved while working in effective schools. There is a large body of educational research literature on effective schooling that documents relationships between an array of school and classroom practices and students' academic and behavioural performance. Focused initially on inner-city elementary schools that serve large numbers of poor children, these studies increase our understanding of how to build a supportive environment for teaching and learning. Researchers have looked at factors that distinguish schools and classrooms with high achieving, appropriately behaving students from those in which achievement and behavioural outcomes are less desirable. Key factors for Lawrence Heights are:

- Time-on-task
  Research on classroom management and on generic instructional strategies has convincingly demonstrated that—at least for the kinds of learning goals measured by conventional standardized tests—teaching approaches that maximize students' time-on-task are likely to enhance their achievement. The point may seem obvious but it is easy to overlook the fact that in classrooms serving disadvantaged children, there are many potential distractions from academic work.
- Establish high expectations and a school climate that supports academic learning
  High expectations for the achievement of all children, active instructional leadership, and a school climate that insures a high priority for academic learning increase the academic performance of students.
- Strengthen the involvement of parents in support of instruction
  Research on the involvement of parents in instruction has led to another insight that corresponds with common sense: students' learning can

be greatly enhanced when parents are actively involved in support of their children's instruction. Although many things constrain the role that parents on low-incomes can play in their children's education, numerous examples attest to the powerful influence of parents when they become involved with learning (with or without the active encouragement of the school).

By maximizing students' engagement in learning, creating a school climate that supports academic learning and involving parents in the education of their children, schools that serve disadvantaged children can accomplish a great deal. While these improvements establish a foundation for academic learning, they have little to do with the nature of what is taught and how it is taught.

Whom We Teach

A great deal of research and practice has been predicated on the assumption that "disadvantaged" students arrive at school with cognitive, experiential and linguistic deficits. Such deficits are thought to derive from the family and community situations of these students. By focusing first on what they perceive to be students' deficits, educators risk making inaccurate assessments of children's strengths and weaknesses and overlooking their true capabilities. For example, teachers have been known to interpret dialectal speech patterns as decoding errors. Educators who have low expectations for disadvantaged students may set standards that are not high enough to form the foundation for future academic success.

A growing body of research (Knapp and Associates 1995; Letgers, McDill and McPartland 1993), as well as the experience of many educators who work with disadvantaged children, provides a conception of these students that can help teachers avoid the adverse consequences of the deficit model. This alternative perspective begins with the simple assumption that all students arrive at school with their own ways of speaking and interacting with adults and peers, and with ideas about the purpose of schooling and the likelihood of their success. Understanding these individual characteristics can help educators to explain how students interpret and react to what takes place in the classroom. For many students, the skills, experiences and behaviour patterns they have learned outside of school are readily applicable to the demands and routines of the school day. For other students the skills and strategies they have acquired to get along in their own communities prove to be ineffective when it comes to meeting the demands of the school setting.

From this perspective, some students are doubly disadvantaged: first due to their patterns of behaviour, language use and values not matching those required in the school setting; second, by teachers and administrators who fail to diagnose and address their particular difficulties and to take advantage of the strengths that these students do possess. Over time these phenomena can create a cycle of failure and despair that culminates in students turning their backs on school and dropping out.

This same line of research also suggests that the cycle of failure and despair can be broken—or need not even begin—if educators take steps to minimize the incongruities between schools and students' homes. Such steps include developing instructional programs that incorporate the life experiences and skills that students bring to the classroom and at the same time providing students with the skills and strategies they will need to succeed in the larger society. This approach implies that teachers need to know and respect the cultural and linguistic backgrounds of students and that they communicate this respect to students in a personal way. At the same time, it suggests that teachers, as they explain and model the dimensions of academic learning, should make explicit to these students the assumptions, expectations and way of doing things in school—in short, the school culture (Knapp, Turnbull and Shields 1990: 2–8).

How We Teach

The most widely accepted strategies for teaching children from disadvantaged backgrounds emphasize teacher directed instruction and the use of homogenous whole-class or small-group formats. Such approaches help to maintain order in the classroom—no small feat in many classrooms with large numbers of children. These and other commonly used strategies allow the teacher to structure learning tasks, monitor progress, maintain momentum and minimize distractions efficiently. By grouping students who are at similar levels of attainment, teachers can target instruction more closely to their particular needs and skills. For these reasons, this approach to instruction lends itself well to skills-based, sequential curricula.

There are several things that typically do not happen in such classrooms and, if the goal is to engage students in challenging and coherent academic work, their absence is troublesome. First, when teachers actively direct all or most aspects of instruction, students tend to assume little responsibility for directing their own learning. At worst, children do only what they are told to do and never think about what they are doing, what something means, how to solve a problem sensibility, or how one task relates to another. Second, tight control and rapid pacing of instruction by the teacher leave little room for unstructured interaction among students. Children thus have little opportunity to use one another as resources for learning. Third, although grouping by ability solves some instructional problems, it generally limits low-achieving students' exposure to high-achieving students who can model effective learning. Instead, low-achieving students have only one another to observe and imitate. All too easily low-achieving individuals can be considered to be on a permanent track.

Alternative approaches exist that strike a balance between teacher-directed and student-directed learning that enable children to use one another as learning resources and that avoid the negative effects of permanent tracking. To accomplish these goals, teachers can add various strategies to their instructional repertoires in mathematics, reading and writing. Teachers can:

- provide numerous opportunities for teacher/student and student/student discussion about mathematical ideas and their applications, about the meaning of what has been read and about the meaning of what students write;
- use project-based or team-learning activities, especially those that employ heterogeneous grouping;
- teach explicitly (e.g., by modeling, demonstrating or explaining) the strategies by which students can monitor their own comprehension, tackle unfamiliar mathematics problems on their own, or carry through writing assignments from the inception of an idea to the completion of a polished draft (thus enabling students to carry out extended tasks under their own direction);
- set up supplemental instruction arrangements (for students who need extra help) that are flexible and integrated into regular classroom instruction whenever possible; and
- allow classroom order to reflect the nature of the academic task at hand— within the bounds of reasonable discipline—rather than maintain tight and consistent control throughout (Knapp, Turnbull and Shields 1990: 2–8).

I have long been intrigued with Marva Collins who, after fourteen years of teaching in the troubled Chicago public school system, decided to open her own school on the second floor of her home. The outstanding results generated from that decision have been chronicled in countless newspapers, on CBS 60 Minutes and a made for television movie, The Marva Collins Story. Her style of teaching is grounded in the development of reading skills through phonics, memorization and recitations, and the acknowledgement and praise for work well done. Her successful work with poor, urban children is based on the assumption that all children can learn. As Marva Collins says, "If the student didn't learn it, then I didn't teach it" (Collins 1992: 9).

Chapter 2

Walk the Talk

Philosophically Speaking

My mission as a principal is to bring a vision of dynamic and collaborative leadership to the challenge of public education. The intent of this vision is to build and maintain strong relationships and to encourage commitment and loyalty through trust, growth through participation and responsibility through accountability. My primary function as the principal is to continually acquire, as well as continually teach those being guided, individually and collectively, the attitudes, beliefs, values, knowledge and skills that facilitate success and move students and staff to higher levels of performance.

Peter Drucker (1997: 174), author of *Managing for the Future,* says "the foundation of effective leadership is thinking through the organization's mission, defining it and establishing it clearly and visibly." One of my first challenges as a school leader is to provide opportunities for my staff to discuss their understandings of the Toronto District's School Board's (TDSB) and Lawrence Heights' values, expectations and directions. I also seek confirmation from all partners of our shared responsibility to be of service to our students. At Lawrence Heights we will accomplish this by aspiring to "Provide, promote and support environments that result in world class learning." We believe that all children can learn, and our vision is one that provides students with the tools to be successful. Our vision requires that parents, staff and the community are all engaged in determining the best strategies to impact student learning.

The Toronto District School Board Mission and Values Statement makes a clear commitment to enabling all students to reach high levels of achievement and to providing environments that encourage students to achieve at their own pace. These environments must enable students to apply their academic skills to real life situations. Learning must be inclusive so that every student receives appropriate instruction by means of rich, engaging curricula that respects diversity. This can be achieved in supportive environments that promote high academic achievement, encourage innovation and reward excellence.

The essential characteristics of these environments are: Focus, mission and vision; high academic expectations; collaboration (administration, teachers, students, parents); participation, connectedness, a sense of belonging and a positive school climate; relevance and integration; monitoring, reinforcement and feedback; and a safe and orderly environment.

The only way a school gets better is if the people inside it get better. This is the thinking behind the Toronto District School Board's values statement: we promote and model high standards of performance, encourage risk taking and provide opportunities for staff to learn and grow as individuals and as members of a team. We start each school year with some common understandings around professional development sessions for staff and the need in all program areas to have an emphasis on instruction and assessment. We mentor staff to help them further develop themselves by determining performance objectives and areas of growth. Determining the needs of staff is done by the staff collaborating with school leaders, using data (perception surveys) and aligning their objectives with Board and our family of schools' targets. The overall goal is to improve student achievement.

Partnerships with other supporters of teaching and learning are essential. We seek to establish alliances with business, labour and industry as these partnerships help us understand what skills are needed in the workplace. We also benefit from business or industry funding programs. The fiscal pressures we face are real. The province's new funding formula continues to have a dramatic impact on the delivery of service to our students.

The kind of partnership I like to see grow is the school's partnership with parents. The role of parents within the education system must be strengthened. We must provide meaningful opportunities to put the public back in education. When speaking to parents I remind them of the fact that student achievement is clearly linked to parental involvement.

It is our intention at Lawrence Heights to "develop and maintain a leadership style that is based on teamwork, trust, communication, commitment and competence" (Principal's Values Statement).We invest in our staff by being attuned to issues related to morale, well being and job satisfaction. These factors can affect job performance. Efforts are made to ensure that the workplace becomes a model of excellence in human relations and productivity.

Experience tells me that most people do not care how much you know, they want to know how much you care. Trust tends to be built with staff when they see you are basing your decisions on information collected from people at all levels of the organization. Such a process makes people feel respected and that their views are valued. Even listening to others helps you gain a level of acceptance.

Providing and receiving accurate, up-to-date information on a regular basis also build positive work relations. It is vital that we keep each other informed of our plans and progress, and take advantage of the wealth of expertise and viewpoints of our employees, parents, students and community. We value thoughtful opinions that have the potential to improve student achievement and encourage staff, parents and community members to share them with us. We are committed to being open, accessible and visible in our school. Establishing two-way communication is one of our biggest challenges, but also one of the most important components of a student-focused education partnership.

Public education is perhaps the most important investment our country can provide. It is an entitlement and society's fulfillment of its promise to its children and future generations. To "ensure customer satisfaction and confidence in public education" (TDSB Values Statement) we must continually ask ourselves, "are our customers satisfied?" That is where accountability begins and ends, and it starts with me. For us at Lawrence Heights it means that information must be available to the public, to taxpayers, in a form that allows people to make reasonable judgements about how well the system has performed and to know who is responsible if they are not satisfied. We must ensure that quality, service and results do not remain slogans, but that they permeate all we do.

Student Centred Education

Middle school students are unique and have specific needs in relation to their intellectual, physical, social, emotional, cultural and moral development. Our philosophy at Lawrence Heights reflects a firm commitment to meeting the students' needs in a supportive atmosphere during their transitional years.

Our primary goals are to foster the development of each student's whole personality during this most influential time in his or her adolescence; to guide them toward becoming young adults who have a positive self-image; and to ensure they are capable of coping with and contributing to our complex society. To achieve these goals, a student centred approach is necessary so that the student is first and foremost with a comprehensive curriculum built outwards and evolving around the student. In developing the school-specific curriculum, the needs of the student are continually assessed and considered.

Discipline is always a priority because of its importance to learning. Staff work cooperatively to manage and mould positive student behaviour. This year we added a program to help students solve problems before administrative involvement becomes necessary. Twelve students and two teachers were selected to participate in conflict resolution training. The students act as peer mediators to help other students resolve conflicts. Though still in its infancy, we anticipate the program will have positive results.

No amount of change in schools will produce significant results unless the social needs of middle school students are taken seriously. No amount of clever delivery of subject matter will capture the imaginations and energies of students who feel that their opportunities for social development lie elsewhere. While many of us know better, the organization of our schools currently embodies the belief that students' social needs and activities are incompatible with learning. But individuals learn when the information is relevant to them and the communities that matter to them. People learn in order to know how to be productive in their community and to gain access to valued forms of community participation. Their rewards are seeing their contribution, knowing others recognize their contribution and forging a new sense of themselves.

This does not mean that schools should build their curriculum around rap videos or video games. School curriculum should provide students with meaningful opportunities to connect their school work with their lives and to express themselves through participation in learning activities. If students are to apply what they learn in school into the rest of their lives, they must be able to bring what they learn elsewhere into the school. Currently, the only avenue for developing an identity around learning in the traditional school is through test performance. The primary avenues for expressing creative social activity are disruptive behaviour, lateness, violence and apathy.

In pursuit of this ideal educators need to establish a tradition of innovation. We need to identify new ways to apply our knowledge of youth to teaching, new ways to reach out to our diverse communities, new ways to help parents help their children, new ways to think about learning and new ways of structuring our schools. There needs to be a re-energized focus on the students as central in the mission of education. Educators are realizing that in order to become more student centred we must move from a focus on different types of learners to a focus on individual learners with individual social needs. The more we learn about our students, the more we can shape our courses of study to nurture and respond to their abilities and appetites at each stage of their development.

Our Boys to Men/Project Pride and Sisterhood programs at Lawrence Heights strive to give a voice to participants. A person's voice is the result of her or his lived experiences; it reflects a person's language, culture, gender, race and class. The programs also address issues related to role models, transition to manhood or womanhood, identity/self-esteem, collaboration and safety.

Our school operates from a conviction that all students can learn successfully. We have established a set of twenty-first-century student learning goals that are reflected in our mission and vision statements. A dominant part of our approach is to provide students with an education that is tied to their lives and life skills, including the application and use of technology.

Chapter 3

If it is Educationally Sound
it is Administratively Possible

Summer School and Term 1: September–November

Summertime

JULY 5

Summer school began at Lawrence Heights today. The majority of the students are from our school. Some of the feeder school students are still reluctant to attend our summer school because of our reputation as a school of thugs. Oh well ... more spots for our students. We encourage our students to attend summer school even if they are doing okay. It is only a half-day for three weeks, but this keeps their minds active. I read that most students lose anywhere from three to four months of schooling in the summer, mainly due to intellectual inactivity. This is the case at Lawrence Heights; many of our students will not go to the library, visit a museum or even pick up a book over the summer. To address this concern, we require that returning students complete a summer learning package consisting of language arts, math, social studies and science. The incentive offered to students who complete the package is a guaranteed spot when we go to *Oh Uh* (a popular kids game show) on YTV. It was a huge success when we went last year. So far only one parent has complained.

JULY 6

Just after the mid-morning break at summer school I call Nevan and Russ down to the gym. They have been trash talking one another about who's got game. I suggest that they settle it on the court. Russ, the more vocal of the two, gets lit up 7–0 and 11–4. He refuses to leave the gym. A number of times I calmly ask him to leave, but he is not moving. I don't allow myself to get into a power struggle with him—I walk out of the gym. He later confronts me wondering why he is no longer going to Butch Carter's Basketball Camp.

JULY 8

What a disappointment. Another teacher and I have to drive out to Scarborough to inquire about the students who went to Butch Carter's Basketball Camp on a summer scholarship. Rumour has it they were misbehaving and tried to steal some towels. The camp coordinator confirms the stories. We pull all ten of them into a room at the camp and give them a good old tongue-lashing. You know, the typical stuff about being an ambassador for the school and recognizing the opportunity they have been given. We are prepared to pull all of them out of the camp, but are talked out of it by the coordinator who says they have straightened up and are doing well. We only let it go after the students agree to apologize.

JULY 12

On the way to school I have to make a stop at the florist. One of our school pets, Cyrus, is going to be put down. His owner, Zo, an outstanding teacher on staff, is feeling the pain. She hasn't had much luck with her dogs lately. This is the second one she will lose in the last year. Cyrus is a part of the school's pet project, which provides students with the opportunity to care for a pet. In addition to Cyrus we have a ferret, cat, rat and hamster. The kids just love having them around, and looking after them really teaches students responsibility. Cyrus has such a great temperament. He has been great with the kids and truly loves being around them. I'll miss Cyrus and his morning routine of coming to my office to get his milk bone.

JULY 18

It's a girl! My wife and I celebrate the birth of Briana Juli Spence. She is beautiful and healthy, what more could we ask for?

JULY 23

Summer school is now finished. We had a good summer. The students remained focused for the most part under some tough conditions (no air conditioning). The staff was terrific as usual and later we will celebrate at my place with a barbecue. We finish the day with a recognition assembly for the students. It is a tradition at Lawrence Heights to celebrate the students' successes with medals of learning. Lawrence Heights students are well represented at the assembly. The staff also put their undefeated record on the line with a pick up basketball game against some of the teaching assistants and volunteers. On this day they got the win, but we'll be back. More importantly, everyone has a great time watching and cheering.

JULY 26

For the second straight summer, Bob Maydo (a teacher and basketball coach at Bathurst and a friend) and I host the Star Search Basketball Skills

Development Camp for kids in the neighbourhood. It is our way of giving back to the community. Many of the kids in the area want desperately to attend a basketball camp in the summer but have limited resources. This camp meets that need. We have about fifty kids in attendance and provide basketball skills development, a snack, a T-shirt and lots of fun. The camp is open to boys and girls eleven to fourteen years old. Some of the instructors, like Wayne Smith, who is on a basketball scholarship at Duquesne University, Joseph Asante from Brandon University and Steve Morrison from Weber State University, are from the area. The kids love hanging with those guys just as much as the instructors love hanging with the kids.

August 4

This year we sent almost forty kids to summer camp as part of a scholarship program. We picked up the cost for students to attend a young inventors camp, soccer, basketball and track and field camp. Today, I check on the students at the York University Basketball Camp. They are excited to see me and appear to be having a great time.

August 10

Today I am taking Russ and a couple of other students out for lunch. We need to talk about what went wrong toward the end of the last school year, and what they need to do to be more successful. Russ in particular has had a lot of difficulties. He was given the opportunity to attend a basketball camp on the condition that he attend summer school. That lasted for all of one day. He is a very talented young man but simply has difficulty focusing. If we can reach him it will be a blessing because he is a leader. Russ is going into grade 7 and his peers fear him and respect him. He is a gifted athlete who cannot keep it together long enough to participate on any school team.

This afternoon Ross is polite and positive about the upcoming year. He speaks candidly over some Kentucky Fried Chicken about wanting to lead the basketball team to the championships and about performing with the choir. It is as if the school year that just passed did not even exist. He understands he needs to exercise better self-control and pay more attention to his academics if he is going to be successful. The hook for him is basketball so we shoot a few hoops on my driveway court and talk. He is responsive and accepts his responsibility. After a couple of hours of eating, watching videos and playing ball, we call it a day. He seems to appreciate my interest and the day.

August 8

A parent calls in the late evening needing some money. She needs a little something to cover costs until payday. I take her account number and will deposit some funds in the morning.

AUGUST 14

Tom, a close friend and colleague on staff (the guidance counsellor), calls me. He is very distressed. He has just learned that three of our students have been arrested. I can sense the sadness and anger in his voice. He has invested so much time and money in one of the students, and now this. I do my best to reassure him that it is not his fault and he has done all he can, but he's hurting right now. We share some of our successes at school this year and he begins to come around. He is very passionate about what he does and gives so much. He doesn't deserve this.

AUGUST 18

Dr. Marine, a celebrated musician and producer, has been actively involved in resurrecting our music program for the last couple of years and has done a marvelous job. Today, we meet to discuss the upcoming year. She has a concert song package prepared for us to discuss that includes Motown, opera and gospel. The students love and respect Dr. Marine and she always gets the most out of them. Last year the choir performed in Windsor, Detroit, Buffalo and around metro Toronto. They also had appearances on CBC and City TV. We are so proud of them.

Dr. Charmaine Marine

AUGUST 19

I meet with Dana, from our primary feeder school, to discuss the upcoming year. They are coming off a terrific year in which they won a national education award from the National Quality Institute (NQI). The NQI is a not-for-profit organization that provides focus and direction for Canadian organizations to achieve excellence. We plan to work together and build an even stronger partnership between our staffs and students. We hope to implement a professional development session for staff on emotional intelligence. On my way home I stop at the school board's central office to drop off a package of articles to be copied for staff. I am really interested in sharing the articles on emotional intelligence and how it can be instrumental in the staff's and students' success.

AUGUST 20

They say that breakfast is the most important meal of the day. I am concerned that many of our students don't eat breakfast and as a result have difficulty focusing on their academics. Last year we started a PowerSnack program which ensures that every student and staff in the school has a nutritious snack. It works well and the students and staff enjoy the mid-morning break to re-energize. This year we want to do more by providing two morning snacks, one at 8:45 and the other at 10:25. I meet with the cafeteria manager for our school and the food services manager for the school board to explore the possibilities. They are both receptive and excited about the idea.

AUGUST 24

While I am out for a run my wife, Marcia, takes a call from a Montreal police officer. He requests that I give him a call and leaves a case reference number. The case is a sexual assault disclosure that a student made during the last school year. The assault took place when she was just ten years old.

AUGUST 31

Our new superintendent calls a meeting with principals and vice principals from our family of schools to set some parameters for the upcoming year. Issues such as when we will meet and the agenda are discussed. It is suggested that a steering committee be set up to look into the agenda items. She tells us about herself and her philosophy on education. I look forward to working with her. The administrative team from our school is introduced to the new vice principal at our local high school.

SEPTEMBER 1

We are very concerned about Steve and Sandy, two students who are returning to our school this fall. Steve is going into grade 7 and Sandy is going into grade 8. They also happen to be brother and sister. I offer to take them and their mother to lunch to talk about the upcoming school year and our expectations. We head over to McDonald's and have a burger for lunch. I sense a real cold shoulder from Sandy, who clearly cannot stand to be in my presence. After we eat I explain my concerns, first with Sandy and then with the Steve. Sandy begins to come around a bit with the help from her mother, who insists I am only trying to help. Sandy's mother lets her know that her body language is so bad it really sends a negative message. Sandy tries unsuccessfully to change it over lunch.

Their mother makes it very clear that she is fed up with her children's poor behaviour and that she wants to see changes. Both of her children spent the last few weeks of school at home, unable to meet the school's expectations. She is far more concerned with Steve, who is seemingly disrespectful and out of control at home.

We decide what needs to happen this year and everyone agrees to it. Steve will remain in a behaviour program and Sandy will be placed with a teacher she thinks she can be successful with. They have both exhausted the staff's support, which has been extraordinary for both of them. They appear to understand that more difficulties will result in their transfer to an alternative school.

SEPTEMBER 3

Staff have been in the school all week. They are excited and ready to go. Just some fine tuning of class lists and timetables still to do. Students and parents have been calling. They are wondering if the uniforms are in yet. This is the first year for standard uniforms for our students and the orders will be ready for pick-up tomorrow.

SEPTEMBER 4

It's about 7:00 p.m. and my wife, our daughter and I take a ride to the school. The staff and students have been very good to us. They made a beautiful toy box for our little girl and have brought over gifts for her. I tape up a thank you card for everyone to see on Tuesday morning when they arrive. I also stuff everyone's mailbox with a loot bag of goodies and a card expressing my thanks and hopes for the upcoming school year. It is going to be a GREAT year.

Strong leadership appears in virtually every list of attributes of successful schools. How do leaders engage teachers, families and communities in partnerships to build programs that meet the needs of their students? I believe that effective leaders consider the contributions of every staff member and what each person can bring to the table to help their students meet the challenges of the curriculum. Therefore leaders must hear the voices of many stakeholders and see that a collective vision for the school is crafted collaboratively, with the students as the focus.

Fall Term

SEPTEMBER 7

Opening day at Lawrence Heights is outstanding. The students look incredible in their uniforms. We have started a uniform program at the school this year for some very good reasons. Before long all public school students in Ontario may be wearing uniforms. Before implementing the program I did some research and conducted a needs assessment (see Appendix A).

There are numerous ambitious initiatives currently underway in Ontario that aim to reform public education. In city after city, the reports of underachievement, disorder and violence are rampant. Convinced that the structure of public education contributes to its ineffectiveness in educating a large proportion of students, imaginative leaders are implementing systemic changes. Reformers are convinced that schools cannot function the way they used to, when superintendents instructed principals, principals instructed teachers, teachers instructed students and parents expected their children to mind what they were told.

The reforms that are now being enacted by many boards of education are intended to incorporate such principles as diversity, quality and accountability. Reformers seek a system in which academic standards are the same, rather than a system that regulates identical schools. The bottom line is, are children learning? Is there more we could be doing to improve student outcomes?

In exploring these questions, public school systems across Ontario may soon be experimenting with or considering policies that call for the use of school uniforms or stricter dress codes. The provincial government recently said the province is considering enforcing a dress code because it believes students learn better without the distractions of fashion.

The very idea of uniforms appeals to a lot of parents and teachers. They are seen as a concrete and visible means of restoring order in classrooms. Uniforms conjure up visions of schools that are safe, secure and orderly learning environments. But are uniforms such a great idea, especially in today's schools which theoretically celebrate diversity rather than uniformity? Are they just a fad?

How would people feel if their local school board proposed school uniforms? Would it relieve a lot of the tension that arises in households over what can be worn to school? Do people believe dress codes would enhance students' academic performance? Would school uniforms stifle children's creativity and ability to express personality through dress? Uniforms and strict dress codes have both critics and supporters.

Critics complain that uniforms and strict dress codes lessen a student's individuality and offer a simplistic approach to preventing school violence. Some educators have suggested that any form of dress code or uniform takes away students' freedom of expression and thereby infringes on their rights.

On the other hand, proponents believe they have an overwhelming case in favour of the use of uniforms. They believe that uniforms help sharpen kids' focus on the task at hand—schoolwork—instead of on what they wear. Uniforms emphasize that the purpose of attending school is learning, not making a fashion statement. Many families recognize the immediate benefit of not having to buy so many expensive clothes for their fashion conscious children.

Uniforms should be presented to students and parents not as a reaction to problems, but rather as a proactive plan to develop a sense of school pride and connectedness. Effective schools are characterized by a sense of pride on the part of the students. School logos and mascots have historically connected students to their school. An important part of adolescence is the opportunity to affiliate with the community of their school. Uniforms are another concrete way to accomplish this.

Any kind of educational reform should be about equity and high academic standards. It is about doing things that engage students in their schooling. I believe that to reach these higher academic levels and address the whole child, students must be in an environment that is sensitive to their developmental needs. They need to be treated fairly and with respect, to receive age appropriate, challenging instruction and to be held accountable for their dress, behaviour and schoolwork.

If student uniforms can help to deter school violence, promote discipline and foster a better learning environment, then we should explore their implementation in our schools. This debate is not likely to go away soon. School administrators, students and parents have to decide whether uniforms will help reform our schools and improve educational performance. Community members need to understand that our schools are seeking new ways to help students become more successful learners. We need to hear from all these people in order to shape the vision and set goals and plans for our schools.

About a half dozen former students dropped by to say hello. They miss being here.

I have a bit of a reputation as a memo maniac. I routinely send out memos to staff, but today I limit my memos to one and it is addressed to the convenors. I have asked them to advise their teams that daybooks are mandatory. I just think it is good planning to have an idea where you are going with your students on a daily, weekly and long-range basis. I was concerned last year with the gaps in planning, particularly when a supply teacher was coming in. Hopefully, daybooks will alleviate that concern.

SEPTEMBER 8

Things are going really well. We have our first school-wide assembly and outline the expectations and goals for the 1999–2000 school year. I pay particular attention to school-wide discipline, which is still a concern. I distribute to staff a memo and some documents regarding discipline.

The key to effective discipline is a shared vision among students, teachers, parents and administrators about what is acceptable, appropriate behaviour in a school setting. This shared vision must be communi-

Table 2: Non-Attendance Figures for the 1998 and 1999 School Years

	1998	1999
Office Referrals	351	200
Students sent home	152	75
Lates	1289	999

cated to students weekly. At Lawrence Heights we use weekly grade assemblies—assemblies of all students in a particular grade—to accomplish this.

We work hard at collecting data in our school. We chart everything from office referrals to suspensions and then disaggregate the data. We try to devise programs and policies to address areas of concern. I find the students to be very interested in the number crunching that we try to do. At the assembly the students reacted to how many lates we had last year (1289) and the number of students we sent home (152) with looks and sighs of disbelief.

We set extremely high academic, athletic and social goals for the school. The students love it when we set goals like repeating as basketball champs or winning a team medal in track and field, or having five successful dances. At the assembly I remind them that we have all the talent right here in the gym to attain all the goals we have set. However, students need to do their part—their part is coming to school every day ready to learn.

I am convinced that the staff of Lawrence Heights are in a league of their own. I tell the students to make some noise and recognize the teachers who will be working with them every day to make them better students. It is a great assembly that ends with a video I produced that captures some of the magic moments at school last year such as the Arts and Literacy Gala, the Motown Review, student reflections on what is the best thing about Lawrence Heights and a visit to the school by Toronto Raptor Dee Brown. Students and staff enjoy the video and demonstrate their appreciation with a rousing applause.

Any time the police show up at the school I get really concerned. Fortunately, they are only here to pick up Yolanda, a student who is going to testify in court. She witnessed a robbery. We call home to inform her parents of the development and they are concerned that once released the accused may come after her. The police officer is sensitive to her concern and reassures the mother that everything will be okay, and away Yolanda goes.

It's 6:30 p.m. and I am just about ready to leave when I get a phone call from a parent. She is disturbed by the fact, and rightfully so, that her daughter was robbed of her bus tickets by a student from our school. He grabbed her pouch and took the bus tickets out of it. I am so disappointed, but I will reserve judgement until we investigate further. We have worked

Toronto Raptor, Dee Brown, visits.

so hard to change the negative image of our school, and now this. Tomorrow morning I will call a grade 6 assembly and get to the bottom of this. This incident reminds me that we need to start some of the social/emotional programs we began last year, like Boys to Men, Sisterhood and Project Pride.

The academic and social underachievement of Black male students in our school continues to be a concern. Many factors have been cited for their underachievement, including economics, parents, community and the environment. Effective schools research (Edmonds 1979a) makes it clear that whatever influence is exerted by these factors, schools can make a difference.

The Mid-Atlantic Equity Centre (Denbo 1997) has identified essential characteristics of effective instruction, which include:

Learning to Persist/Persisting to Learn:
This assists teachers in improving the academic self-concept of minority students by asking teachers to: 1) Understand why some students fail to successfully complete a task; 2). Identify non-persisting students; and 3) Pinpoint curriculum and instructional strategies that can help students learn to persist. Persistence is a learned behaviour, and students from disadvantaged backgrounds observe adults who lack control of their environment and view luck or chance as a more significant factor in success than effort or persistence.

Cross Cultural Communication—An Essential Dimension of Effective Education:
This section discusses cultural differences that lead to communication problems in the classroom and suggests behaviours that affirm rather than devalue a minority students' culture. Since our educational institutions tend to reflect the norms and values of the majority culture, cultural misunderstandings often have a negative effect on a minority students' academic performance.

Improving Black Student Achievement by Enhancing Students' Self-image:
This helps teachers to better understand the factors that contribute to a positive self-image for Black students and to design and implement instructional strategies that will enhance Black students' academic self-concept. While a positive academic identity is important for all students, it is a particularly critical issue for underachieving Black students.

Recognizing the need to provide extra support to our Black students, Project Pride is born. I send a memo on Project Pride to all staff members.

Project Pride Mentors

Memo
To: All staff
From: Chris Spence
Re: Project Pride

Introduction
The present, well-documented crisis in the Canadian education system is experienced first-hand by African-Canadian males. The crisis is revealed in part by multiple statistical parameters including low test scores, suspensions, office referrals, lates and dropout rates. According to social psychologist Claude Steele, "the underachievement of these students stems not from limitations in their innate ability to achieve and to succeed in school, but from systemic discrimination which erodes their self esteem and makes them feel alienated from achievement in school, as a means of protecting their self worth. This alienation allows them to appear unaffected by their academic failure, insulates them from the failure of academic life, confers an illusion of invulnerability, but leads inevitably to more failure."

Objective
The objective of Project Pride is to emphasize the need for African-Canadian males in our school to assume personal responsibility for their own circumstances. It is intended to challenge them to succeed academically and to provide leadership for their families, communities and school. This program is about pride, dignity and respect. It's about saying no to crime, drugs, violence and academic failure.

Methodology
Staff members will identify twenty African-Canadian academically and socially at-risk male students for the program. Once a working group of students and staff members is established, parents/guardians will be notified of the program, and selected participants will meet with their mentors to discuss the mission of the program. Each participant will then be assigned a mentor who will undertake the following tasks:

- daily communication with the student
- weekly communication with the home (minimum of two phone calls with parent or student per week)
- monitoring of homework completion, assignment completion, test preparation and school related assignments
- liaison between the student and staff members

- develop an educational and personal plan for the participant
- ad hoc meetings as the need arises

Conclusion

It is to our credit at Lawrence Heights that we recognize the deep emotional and academic crisis experienced by the African-Canadian males at our school. The crisis confronting these males is intense, and the need for them to reclaim their own dignity and self-respect is obvious. We need to tell them to start thinking about laying the groundwork for the next millennium. We need to tell them to find another mountain to climb or planet to walk on, and to be a part of something that will forever change the world.

To achieve the objectives of Project Pride we need to establish a tradition of innovation—new ways to apply our knowledge of youth to teaching and new ways to reach out to our diverse communities. We must believe we can change things, otherwise what is left to believe in? What can sustain us if we believe that we have no power to make all students at Lawrence Heights successful?

SEPTEMBER 9

Another loan to a parent until the 20th. I keep telling myself that I am going to stop doing this. A day of cards for me—one from a student thanking me for the opportunity to attend a track camp in the summer and one from a summer school administrator, also thanking me for a great summer. It is little things like that, that brighten my day.

I call a grade 6 assembly to investigate the alleged incident where a student was robbed of her bus tickets. No one can confirm the little girl's story. In fact the only thing witnesses can confirm is that she hit the accused student over the head with a binder. Nonetheless all involved are given a stern talking to and parents are notified. It is important to process this initially in front of the other grade 6 students just so they know that we take these kinds of allegations very seriously. The two individuals involved eventually leave my office with smiles on their faces and their dignity intact.

Steve and Sandy missed the first day of school, but once they arrive their presence is known. I speak with their core teachers and ask them to remind them of our meeting over the summer and the thin ice that they are skating on.

It didn't take long—today we have to send a student home for her threatening and disruptive behaviour. Her teacher has been very patient and has dealt with the issues within the classroom, but today is the last straw. Since opening day Yolanda has had an issue every day with a different student. Today she and another student get into a physical confrontation (kicking one another). We suspend her until Monday, while the other student will serve her suspension in the office. These consequences follow the counselling session they receive for behaviour that required referral to the office.

Yolanda's mother arrives at the school a short time later and is angry. She is yelling and causing quite a ruckus in the office. Terri, the vice-principal who made the call home, and I mainly listen and stand our ground. We let her know we are only trying to create a safe school and this was her daughter's third incident in three days. She comes around slightly and leaves with a better understanding of what we are trying to do and how her daughter should have handled the situation.

It seems I haven't spent much time writing about academic issues and that is only because for the first two to three weeks of school my expectations are that staff will thoroughly assess each student in their class and get to know them. To give students the individualized program instruction they need we have to know where they are academically (numeracy and literacy are our focus). The assessment framework below is given to staff.

Assessment is the collecting and analyzing of data and information about a student's achievement. The main purpose of assessment is to improve student learning by identifying students' strengths and weaknesses.

Effective student assessment should:

- measure what it intends to measure
- give an accurate description of what students are capable of doing
- be consistent with curriculum expectations
- accommodate special needs of students
- provide enough information to allow an accurate judgement of student achievement
- be free of bias

Information regarding expectations, assessment methods and results should be communicated to all stakeholders as promptly, clearly and openly as possible.

An assessment profile of every student is due in the office by the end of September. That information becomes very useful when discipline issues arise.

SEPTEMBER 10

In my mailbox today are the minutes from one of the grade team meetings. The focus is academic and on the students—exactly what we want. It is the first year since I have been here that we have been able to provide meeting time on teachers' timetables. If we are going to be a truly collaborative culture this kind of opportunity to plan and share is imperative. Teachers at Lawrence are expected to work together to alter the curriculum and pedagogy within subjects, such as infusing both with an anti-racist perspective. They are expected to make connections between subjects, such as integrating academic and vocational education. The kind of collaboration I am speaking about goes beyond providing advice and feedback to one another.

I believe that teachers who work together see significant improvements in student achievement, behaviour and attitudes. Students can sense program coherence and consistency of expectations, and their improved behaviour and achievement are a reflection of this. Teacher collaboration also breaks the isolation of the classroom, leads to increased feelings of effectiveness and satisfaction, and creates "a more elaborate and exciting notion of teaching" (Popkewitz and Myrdal 1991: 35). For new teachers, this collegiality saves them from the sink or swim, trial and error ordeal. For experienced teachers, collegiality prevents end of the year burnout and stimulates enthusiasm.

In our experience, teachers who work closely together become more adaptable and self-reliant. When working together, they have the energy, organizational skills and resources to attempt innovations that may exhaust an individual teacher. A collaborative environment fosters continuous learning by the teachers and this enhances their effectiveness in the classroom.

The establishment of a leadership team and the involvement of staff in school improvement initiatives vastly increases the collaborative, cooperative, collegial efforts in the school. The leadership team itself represents an opportunity for teachers to work together in a decision-making capacity as they work to move the school through the improvement process. We meet regularly to collect and share data on the school and develop ways the rest of the staff could work together to focus on school improvement. Teachers are directly involved in leading the improvement effort.

The morning gets off to an emotional start when Trent, a grade 7 student, and his mother come into my office. Trent and his mother are both crying. They are both very upset. This is probably the third or fourth time they have come in to talk. Last year I drew up a plan to check and see how he was doing at home that called for weekly communication with his parents.

The difficult part is that the issues are non-school issues. At school Trent is a keen and eager student, who is almost always polite and

Some of the commonly asked questions around school improvement at Lawrence Heights

What data do we use to monitor school improvement?
We analyze two types of data, both of which are crucial to our improvement: "what" data and "why" data.

"What" data is the information that describes current and past levels of student performance such as attendance, EQAO testing, Project 8, and suspensions. "What" data are usually quantitative and help us to identify our focus areas and the goals and objectives of our school plan.

"Why" data is information that identifies possible reasons for achievement being at its current level, such as scheduling and use of time in the school. This kind of data can be qualitative and anecdotal.

How are we using data to improve student achievement?
Summative assessment data (such as EQAO and Project 8) are used to develop measurable goals and objectives in school improvement plans. Such data help our school to set targets that drive school plans and demonstrate progress in student achievement. Results are analyzed carefully by staff and teams of teachers to identify short- and long-term student achievement trends and curriculum development implications.

Formative assessment data are used to identify what students already know and to help teachers focus instruction on the needed skills to improve individual student achievement. Sources of formative assessment include student journals, conferences with students and student observations. This type of assessment helps teachers answer the following questions with more precision:

- What do students know and what do they need to learn next?
- To what extent have students acquired the taught outcomes and indicators of success?

Formative data also identify students who need specific assistance and those who are ready for increased enrichment opportunities.

Note: The Education Quality and Accountability Office (EQAO) is an arm's length agency of the Government of Ontario responsible for increasing accountability and contributing to enhanced quality education in Ontario. Project 8 is our own in-house grade 8 assessment that models the EQAO, which is for grades 3, 6, 9 and 10.

Do The Right Thing

Choices
All of us make choices everyday, some more important than others. In making choices, people may consider what is best for them, what is fair, what is right, what is easy, or a variety of other things. People usually make decisions on the basis of what is important to them. As part of the Boys to Men Program we are encouraging individuals to do the right thing.

Dear Parent/Caregiver:
Please check the appropriate box with regards to your son's weekly decision making.

This week my son was helpful around the house
This week my son spent a reasonable amount of time on his academics
This week my son cooperated with his siblings
This week my son responded to reasonable requests
This week my son came home after school at a reasonable time
This week was a good week at home for my son

respectful. Apparently, today he refused to eat breakfast and walked out of the house. His mother was very upset and disciplined him in front of his friends—a tough thing to swallow for any twelve-year-old. But today's issue is only part of what Trent's mother describes as out of control, disrespectful behaviour. He also is having great difficulty with his sisters. They are continuously fighting and their mother sees him as the instigator.

I mainly listen and try to mediate, and I strongly recommend counselling. The meeting becomes so intense that they are both sobbing and yelling at one another at the same time. I have to get a little more involved and sternly ask them both to BE QUIET! When the crying stops I ask again what I can do to help. The mother is frustrated and asks me to allow her husband to resolve it when he arrives. She wants her son to go home with her right now, but under the circumstances I suggest he stays and she goes. She agrees.

A short time later Trent's father comes to the school. He is calm and pensive about what to do. He is very concerned about the home situation and also thinks his son is out of order. He demonstrates little interest in counselling and is convinced that the only solution is to send Trent back to Eritrea, in East Africa, to gain a sense of his culture and to develop the discipline he needs. We talk further, but his mind is made up.

Terri has done some follow-up on Yolanda, the student we sent home yesterday. She has called the school she attended last year and our concerns are confirmed. Yolanda is an at-risk student who had a very difficult time last year. We are going to have to monitor her progress very closely.

We also need to further examine what conditions predict whether a student will be at risk? What conditions predict the likelihood of a student dropping out of school before graduation, or whether a student will go through high school having a frustrating and unrewarding time?

It was a pleasant surprise to arrive at home and find a beautiful gift basket from my superintendent (Karen Forbes) for our daughter.

The superintendent has recently requested our school plan and portfolio.

At Risk

Researchers have found that it is possible to identify potential dropouts as early as in elementary school (McDill, Natriello and Pallas 1986). Hodgkinson found in his research a widely held view that "we intervene too late in the course of a student's development, that certain parts of the profile of a dropout prone student may be visible as early as the third grade" (Hodgkinson 1985: 12).

There is a great variety of conditions associated with being at risk. Researchers who have investigated characteristics correlated with a high likelihood of dropping out mention demographic, socio-economic and institutional characteristics such as:

- Being a member of a low-income family,
- Having low academic skills (although not necessarily low intelligence),
- Having parents who are not high school graduates,
- Speaking English as a second language,
- Being single parent children,
- Having negative self-perceptions.

Wehlage and Rutter note that "the most powerful determinants of dropping out are low expectations and low grades combined with disciplinary problems, truancy being the most common offence" (Wehlage and Rutter 1986: 4). They add that while the school can't do much about the socio-economic factors that are associated with being at risk, the things found to be determinants are things that are very much under the school's control.

SEPTEMBER 13

A good day at the Heights—a student from one of our special programs (we have three: educable, learning disabled and behavioural) came down to read some of his writing to me. He was so proud of his work.

I am still a little concerned with Sandy. She appears to be okay today in her core class but every time she comes into contact with another staff member she is disrespectful. I speak to her core teacher and explain my concerns ... again.

Effective administrators are visible in their schools. We try to be out in the halls during class change, lunchtime and before and after school. We also make a point of visiting every classroom at least once a day, just to say hi and browse through a notebook or two. Today, I am particularly warmed by my visit to the library. The students are gathered in a semi circle and are discussing autobiographies. The students are focused and interested. For us this is a huge improvement. I reflect on the time I walked into the library during my first year at the school and students were throwing books out the window!

SEPTEMBER 14

Choir practice starts today bright and early at 7:30 a.m. We have a good turnout of about forty. I strongly believe that music is extremely important to have. We didn't always have a program. The power of music and its relevance to subjects as diverse as history and mathematics suggest that we need more of it at Lawrence Heights. For certain learners, music can be a gateway to knowledge. The sounds of music might communicate meanings more clearly than words.

Learning to play a musical instrument helps students to develop mentally, emotionally and socially. Instrumental practice enhances coordination, concentration, memory and improvement of eyesight and hearing.

The benefits of music have been well documented:

- Music contributes to the school and community environment
- Music makes our days come alive and this, in turn, leads to more learning
- Music combines behaviours to promote a higher order of thinking skills
- Music provides a way of self-expression and creativity
- Music enriches our lives
- Music composing and performing are satisfying and rewarding activities
- Music education builds the sense of self-worth of participants
- Music is a therapeutic outlet
- Music develops intelligence in other areas
- Music provides opportunities for success for some students who have difficulty with other aspects of the school curriculum.

We salute our music teachers because this is one of the programs that is making a difference with our students.

We start the day with a fire drill and there is a lot of room for improvement. Doors and windows are left open and the students' exit from the building is loud. I ask staff to review appropriate fire drill procedures and remind the whole school that we will have another one later this week.

A parent drops by to let us know she loves the uniform. Her son looks and feels terrific. A friend and administrator from a nearby school also drops by and likes what he sees. The tone of the schools is positive. And a parent drops us a note to let us know what a wonderful program PowerSnack is. It provides every student in the school two healthy snacks a day.

Another parent (before my time) drops by to see a staff member and has some staff confused. They remember her as a she, but now she is a he. The story is confirmed: she is now surgically a he. Tomorrow is our staff meeting, which means an early dismissal. We send home a letter reminding parents of significant dates.

September 14

Dear Parent(s)/Guardian(s):

We hope that you had a restful and relaxing summer. This letter is to let you know that we had a very successful opening at Lawrence Heights. The school uniform program has been a success. Many of us have spent countless hours over the summer preparing for this year, as we all want to make this a year to remember. We recognize our students' success will result from establishing high expectations and basic codes of conduct, and from enforcing those standards with diligence and rigour. This cannot be accomplished without an outstanding staff, and you. We are privileged to be amongst a group of educators who are willing to provide a level of commitment, dedication and energy that will keep the students of Lawrence Heights on the road to success.

We look forward to seeing you at the Open House Barbecue on September 23. At the barbecue I will speak to our Parent Pact, which recognizes the education of our students is a shared responsibility.

Parent Pact
Lawrence Heights Middle School is a community of life long learners where staff, parents, students and community work together to ensure academic and social success in a safe learning environment. We seek to empower every student to learn, develop, achieve success and participate responsibly in the diverse technological and global society of the twenty-first century. In our quest to serve our vision, a partnership must exist between home and school. Please take the time to read through and commit to the Parent Pact to ensure the success of your child. The Parent Pact involves:

- Regular school visits and attendance at school events (e.g., a commitment to dropping into the school once a month).
- Daily monitoring and signing of the student planner and regular communication with your son/daughter's teacher.
- Ensuring they have a minimum of one hour of quiet time every evening for homework completion and daily reading. It is highly recommended that parent(s)/guardian(s) read regularly with their son/daughter.
- Monitoring the use of the phone and television.
- Knowing who their friends are.
- Ensuring a reasonable bedtime and wake up time during the school week, to ensure punctuality and attentiveness.

One of the new features of our school is the Parent Reception area, which is located across from the office. Drop in and enjoy a cup of coffee, read the newspaper and find out what is happening in our school. We are also introducing a Parent of the Month program to complement our student of the month program.

Only through the commitment of students, parents and staff can the above be accomplished.

Together We're Better!

Respectfully yours,

Dr. C. Spence

SEPTEMBER 15

A couple of staff members have told me that they are concerned about Mandy, a new student to the school. She has been drawing some morbid pictures (death, blood, etc.) She also talks frequently about killing people, stabbing people and hurting people. We decide to monitor her very closely and arrange a home visit by Tom (guidance counsellor), and then to get the school psychologist to assess her.

While talking to some students in the hall during class change I learn that the reason why some students have been late after lunch is that they are visiting the mall and stealing. I am really concerned because this became a significant issue last year. Some girls stole bathing suits to go on an end of the year trip with their homeroom teacher. I speak to the girls with Terri, the vice-principal, and let them know what we are hearing and our concern.

Miles, a former student, drops by with his parent and a friend. He is trying to get into the local high school and will undoubtedly have some difficulties. His attendance with us last year was sporadic. He had great difficulty meeting the expectations of the school and had to be suspended repeatedly for conduct injurious to the moral of the school. He is looking for a positive reference to get into school. I tell him straight up … no can do. I have to tell it the way it is.

Today is our first staff meeting and we have a full agenda.

At the start the year I always talk a little bit about my philosophy, which is rooted in the belief that all children can learn. I also talk about supporting intelligent people in doing intelligent things with our students, and how I depend on them for the running of the school. I really consider my role to be one of keeping the hope alive.

As we work through the agenda I highlight a few key points, such as my concern that, after having a great year last year let's not cruise, but continue to improve. We must be committed to a cycle of continuous improvement, which requires us to plan, implement, evaluate and report.

I do consider our administrative team to be very flexible, but there are some things that are not open to discussion. These are what I believe are non-negotiables:

> Welcome
> Introduction of new staff
> Philosophy
> Goals for the year
> Focus on students
> Facilitate achievement
> Raise standards
> Ensure equity
> Enhance accountability
> Cruising or moving
> Non-negotiables
> Progress reports
> Games room
> Barbecue
> Convenor report
> Vice-principal report
> Emotional intelligence

- You must attend all staff meetings
- Team planning must be used for that purpose
- You must make use of a daybook
- You must be on duty during scheduled times
- You must submit emergency plans to the office

One of the things that we implemented last year was a bi-monthly progress report to be completed by teachers. It is a simple check system of yes or no on how a student is progressing in her or his studies and life at Lawrence Heights. We are going to continue to use these reports as they provide a useful regular assessment of a student's performance.

This year we are opening up a games room as part of a reward system for our students. Those meeting the expectations and beyond will get the opportunity to play pool, ping pong or some video games.

I end the meeting by handing out a couple of articles, one about the habits of great teachers and the other on emotional intelligence. I am convinced that emotional intelligence—which is just a different way of being smart and includes knowing what your feelings are and using your

If you can't measure it you can't improve it.
A student checking her progress outside the office

feelings to make good decisions—is what will get our learners to the next level.

I receive a late night call from a parent who wants her daughter to be put in a grade 7 class. Presently she is in grade 6, but is age appropriate for grade 7. She was placed a grade behind, apparently because there were some concerns over the gaps in her education. I inform the parent that I will speak to her daughter's teacher who has been assessing all her students.

SEPTEMBER 16

A parent calls asking if there are any job opportunities at the school. He offers to clean staff cars, make clothes, anything to get a few extra bucks. I promise to see what I can do. I feel for the guy, he is a terrific parent.

It makes my day when a staff member is bubbling with enthusiasm when two of his students understand a math concept after visiting a grocery store. He is alarmed, however, that they can't make change or do some simple computations.

A call from Mona, one of our feeder school principals, is cause for concern. An expensive camera is missing after a couple of students from our school paid a visit. I call Reggie, who allegedly stole the camera, down to the office. He says he found it in the field and goes and gets it from his locker. The owner of the camera, a gifted and dedicated teacher who is

Lawrence Heights Middle School — Student Progress Report 2000–2001

"Believing in Achieving"

Student Name_____

Date Issued_____

The information contained in this report represents a summary of the student's performance during the last two weeks.

Since the last report your son/daughter is progressing/not progressing in the following areas:

	Yes	No	Level of Achievement			
English	☐	☐	1	2	3	4
Math	☐	☐	1	2	3	4
Science	☐	☐	1	2	3	4
French	☐	☐	1	2	3	4
Social Studies	☐	☐	1	2	3	4
Visual Arts	☐	☐	1	2	3	4
Phys. Ed.	☐	☐	1	2	3	4
Library	☐	☐	1	2	3	4
Music	☐	☐	1	2	3	4
Drama	☐	☐	1	2	3	4
Family Studies	☐	☐	1	2	3	4
Cooperation with others	☐	☐				
Dressing for success	☐	☐				
Arrives on time for school	☐	☐				
Homework completion	☐	☐				
Parental involvement	☐	☐				
Comments						

Teacher's Signature_____

Parent/Guardian's Signature_____

committed to his students, comes to the school and is upset. He wants to meet with the students who were there, all former students of his. After speaking with them he decides he probably isn't going to get anywhere. Reggie sticks to his story that he found the camera in the field, and no one saw him take it.

I meet with the Literacy Enrichment Academic Program (L.E.A.P.) teachers to discuss the program. L.E.A.P. is for students who:

- have arrived in Canada within the past 60 months
- have shown a significant gap between academic competency and academic functioning
- are functioning academically at the junior division level
- are perceived to have the academic and affective potential to benefit from placement in an intensive academic upgrading in English, mathematics and social studies.

A number of recommendations are made to ensure the success of the program. One is to move their meeting place to a classroom as they are currently working out of the library and an adjoining room.

Today after school we have our first budget meeting. We have a great turnout for the meeting and begin by revisiting last year's budget, and then present this year's.

SEPTEMBER 17

The day starts with a student, Reece, bringing some tasty baked goods for me. I particularly enjoy the banana bread, which is one of my favourites. Later I receive a cute little stuffed animal from one of the students for my daughter. Then the secretaries give us a beautiful gift bag with two gorgeous outfits for my daughter. I am flattered.

A parent drops by to check up on her son, who is off to a terrific start. Another parent drops by to comment on how wonderful the students look going to and from school. She is convinced that the students are much more interested and focused on their schooling since the adoption of the uniform policy.

I receive a call from a cousin of Mandy's, who is concerned about Mandy's behaviour at home. Our hunch is confirmed—this child is at risk. In the past she has been suicidal and has threatened numerous times to call 911 if anyone at home says anything to her that she does not like, such as that she needs to be home at a reasonable hour. She is currently staying with relatives. The Children's Aide Society is involved with the case. Tom sets up a meeting with the family to see what kind of support we can offer them. Right now they feel that the only solution is to send her back to Jamaica.

We are fortunate this year to have more of a guidance program in place than in previous years. I just think it is such an important program to have, especially for middle school learners, who are at an age where they are making crucial decisions about their futures. If they are to make good decisions, they must have good advice.

More and more we are finding that students in our school need someone to listen to, advise, advocate and provide support to them above and beyond their classroom teachers. It is my vision that our guidance program will assist students in achieving optimal development in their personal, social, educational and vocational lives. The program will aspire to provide prevention and intervention through career development; educational development and personal/social development.

For the program to be effective there will need to be excellent, ongoing communication and cooperation between parents and school personnel. The counsellor will regularly meet parents to review student goals and monitor student programs, as well as provide:

- Classroom instruction. The counsellor will provide instruction for students in leadership development and in social/personal/educational development.
- Classroom support. The counsellor will provide lessons on study skills, educational planning, career exploration and secondary options.
- Individual planning. Students will meet with the counsellor to discuss their education plan.
- Response services. The counsellor will be available to deal with personal and educational issues.
- Elementary/Secondary liaison. The counsellor will coordinate and provide information and orientation sessions for grade 5 and 8 students.
- Work connections. The counsellor will coordinate career fair and work experiences for grade 8 students.

Luckily, we have someone on staff who is qualified and perfect for the job. Tom has already started to do home visits and to counsel students.

Terri started a birthday card program last year. It is such an effective way of letting the students know that we care and remember their special day. I was shocked last year to see a couple of our tougher kids inquire as to why they hadn't received their cards yet. The program is up and running and if for some reason we are late with a card the student lets us know.

SEPTEMBER 20

The response to the uniforms has been very positive. Today a parent calls just to say she has seen a real change in her son. For the first time he is talking about going to university. He even gets up early to iron his uniform, and that is something he never used to do.

Well things haven't gotten any better for Sandy. She just doesn't get it. Today I call her mother and explain her latest outburst. Her mother is attentive and interested but seems to have had it with both her kids. I sense the frustration. She tells me Sandy's teacher made a home visit Friday after the outburst in which Sandy was so rude and disrespectful.

She realizes that we are trying to do everything we can to help her daughter be successful.

A counselling session with a grade 6 student and Terri is needed after the student made an inappropriate comment to a teacher about her bra. He appears to be remorseful for the comment, but it doesn't deter us from informing his parents.

Terri chairs a meeting after school about our staff advisor program. All students start and end their day with their staff advisor or home room teacher. The program addresses skills to help students become more independent. There are three areas of focus:

- Student development (academic)
- Interpersonal development (social)
- Career development

A teacher approaches me and is concerned about a student who seems to be masturbating in class. Apparently the student pulls out his shirt and has his hands down his pants. We talk to the student but he is in full denial.

SEPTEMBER 21

Today is a difficult day at Lawrence Heights. I don't know why, but a lot of students are unsettled. We send one student home, Alic, at around 10:00 a.m. because she told the teacher she was talking pure shit. On her way out she slams a few doors and let us know what she thinks about us. This particular student has been tough to reach. She has it in her head that the whole world is against her. These feelings are in spite of everything that we have tried to do for her, like sending her to basketball camp in the summer, providing lunches, arranging outings, etc. I have a good conversation with her mother, who wants to work with us to help her daughter.

Tom returns from a home visit shaking his head about Mandy. Mandy is the same student who has been drawing some morbid pictures. He is now convinced that she may have more than one personality. He briefs me on her history, which is a sad tale of neglect. Tom agrees to have regular contact with the family that is caring for her.

Another student, Yolanda, who had to be sent home already this year, is again referred to the office. This time her comments and actions toward another student at the wrong time (picture day at school) has irked her teacher. Apparently she made another student feel very uncomfortable by making a scene about the girl's body odour.

A couple of other students are referred to the office to resolve a money situation. One student said he gave her the money, while the other student said she took it from him. We put the onus on them to resolve the situation as it has become disruptive to the school.

Another student, Steve, tells a teacher to go fuck himself. This comes after the student was taken to lunch by the same teacher. We are reluctant to suspend the student only because he is having a difficult time at home and is becoming more involved in the street scene. Suspending him is only going to cause more grief because he will be roaming the streets and is certain to find trouble. The teacher does some more counselling. We are not sure where to turn to help this kid. He has exhausted the in-school support and has gone through a treatment centre. He makes a disturbing statement that will stay with us for a long time: "It doesn't matter what you guys do, by the time I'm sixteen I'll be in jail."

Long range plans are to be submitted today. A quick look reveals everyone has paid attention to detail and the new curriculum. Tonight I will look at them more closely.

SEPTEMBER 22

It is a pretty good day at Lawrence Heights. Representatives from YTV visit our school and do a media presentation. The real excitement happens when they hold auditions for the *Uh Oh Show*, a game show for kids with great prizes—lots of fun. It is particularly satisfying to see that some of our students who don't get recognized often are picked to go on the show.

Our superintendent also visits and seems to like what she sees. We talk about an equity and computer project that would see our school (with her assistance) purchase fifty laptop computers that would be available for students to sign out. Too many students at our school don't have access to a computer at home. We also speak about raising some funds for the choir for their trips. Money is an issue and we both agree students should not be excluded because of it.

We welcome Sylvester to our school. Sylvester is a rabbit and is the latest addition to our pet project, which gives students the opportunity to care for a pet.

I speak to a grade 8 class about their lack of homework completion. Homework ensures that students practice, reinforce or apply newly acquired skills and knowledge and learn the necessary skills of independent study. The teacher and I are disappointed that students are not completing homework up to expectations. One of our long-term goals is to set up a homework hotline to provide a source of immediate aid for students and/or parents who are encountering problems when trying to complete homework assignments.

The following are some of the benefits of homework:

* Immediate effects on achievement and learning, including better retention of factual knowledge, increased understanding, better critical thinking

concept formation, better information processing, and curriculum enrichment.

- Long-term academic effects include: learning encouraged during leisure time, improved attitude toward school and better study habits and skills.
- Non-academic long-term effects include: greater self-direction, greater self-discipline, better time organization, more inquisitiveness and more independent problem solving (Walberg et al. 1985: 76–79).

I am saddened that the commotion outside after school is laughter after a female student slips and falls outside. The majority of students that witness the fall are carrying on in a disgusting manner. I really feel for the student. I write a note to myself to address the issue over the announcements tomorrow.

The day ends with a former student dropping by to ask for my help. Apparently, he and a friend went to the local high school to shoot some hoops. Even though they decided not to attend the school they still expect to gain admission to the gym to shoot around. On this day the coach questioned them about their own school and why they weren't playing there. The coach's concern was that the two youngsters, who live in the area but elected to go elsewhere, are going to take away the opportunity to play from others attending the school. Well they didn't like that and told the coach to go fuck himself. That seems to be the phrase of the year when someone says something you don't like.

SEPTEMBER 23

Today is supposed to be our meet the teacher barbecue, but with the threat of rain we decided to postpone the event until next week. I'm really not in the mood for it anyway—we have had a difficult day at school.

Student decision making was at an all time low. The morning starts with a visit from a new female student, Rose, who was beaten up on her way home yesterday. I really feel for her. She is new to the country and a group of girls went out of their way to make her life a living hell. Listening to her tell the story almost brings tears to my eyes. She refused to fight because she had on her uniform and did not want to disrespect the school. She goes on to say that in her country (Kenya) they are taught not to fight, especially when they are in uniform. She was choked and kicked by another student and went home with a bloody mouth. I am not pleased. I have to take a walk before speaking to the perpetrator. When I do, I really let her know how disappointed and angry I am. Reece is usually a pleasure to be around. Her grandmother, who is her primary caregiver, came to the school immediately and is equally disappointed. We suspend her for three days and send her home with enough homework to keep her busy for a while. She also has to apologize to the student, which always seems to be tough for kids. I use the word empathy in my discussions with her as she was in the exact same position last year arriving from Jamaica.

I have written about Mandy who may have multiple personalities. Well Tom in his discussions and investigations tells me there are three personalities: 1) a dead person living inside of her, 2) a happy girl, and 3) a girl who wants sex and drugs. We have started the paper work to get her into a treatment centre. She is having a rough day at school, but home doesn't want her because only the grandmother is home and she fears for her safety.

Sandy and Steve are nearing the end. Every day it gets worse. Especially Sandy who made a comment about Terri and her pregnancy that I can't even repeat—DISGUSTING! The search for an alternative school for her just got intensified.

Overall dress-down day was a nightmare. The day ends with a couple of former students dropping by to visit. A couple of teachers and I sit around and shoot the breeze and have a few laughs. I feel better already. Tomorrow is a new day.

SEPTEMBER 24

Today is a special day for us at Lawrence Heights because a *Toronto Star* reporter came to do a feature on the school. We have two ambassadors greet her at the door and give her a tour of the school showcasing all that we do. Then five of our students, representing each grade, engage in a sit down conversation with her about the school and our policies. This takes place after she has spoken to me about my philosophy. I think it went well but we'll reserve judgement until we see the actual article.

The first progress reports are sent home today. Students who receive all "yes" show them off with a lot of pride as they walk out the door.

A number of students pat me on the back for the no nonsense stance we had to take with Sandy. Anytime students can't learn and teachers can't teach we have a problem.

SEPTEMBER 27

The morning starts with a student, Judy, approaching me with a letter. The letter is a note of apology for her involvement in the beating up of Rose a few days earlier.

We also have to deal with a situation that happens off school property. Len went to the store in his school uniform and stole four bottles of pop and got caught. We talk so much to the students about being an ambassador every time they put on their uniform. Today we are all embarrassed because students from our school will now be painted with the same brush. The grade assembly gives us an opportunity to talk about the situation. In front of his peers the student at fault takes full responsibility for the situation he has created.

I work out a deal with another principal to exchange students who need a change of scenery. Jerry, the student coming our way, was involved in a situation where another student's hair got lit on fire. He says he was just there and not involved. I meet with him and his mother and let them know what the expectations are. He has a pretty good day and seems positive.

The student we have in the wings and ready to go is Sandy. We are going to try one more thing before asking her to leave. Tom, who has been actively involved in this situation, is growing increasingly frustrated by the day. He has done so much for them, but it may be in vain.

We have been lucky to be involved in the Canadian Club Luncheon Series. Last year students got the opportunity to attend a luncheon with P.J. Patterson, the prime minister of Jamaica. Today the guest speaker is Rick Hansen. The eleven students and staff that go really enjoy the afternoon.

I am saddened to get a phone call from my sister, also a teacher (elementary school). She informs me that there was a shooting in her school yard today. Luckily, none of the students is injured but they were out there for recess. The dispute is between some older guys in the community.

SEPTEMBER 28

Now that the dust has cleared a little I am better prepared to speak to Steve and Sandy's parent. Sometimes I think people forget that we have feelings as well. No matter what anyone says, the horrible comments that are sometimes directed at us do hurt. Wishing that I were dead, and a host of other things that I can't even repeat, are hurtful comments. Anyway, I speak to Sandy's parent and let her know that this is the final proposition for her daughter, who will now be on a modified schedule. The parent agrees to the schedule and understands the next step is a new school. I have already made arrangements for her at another school in a behaviour program. The other options that we have investigated are not well received by Sandy's mother. She has gone through the treatment alternative with her son with little success. The other programs require the student to take some responsibility for her or his actions and to want to attend the program. Sandy refuses to do that.

I receive a gift from a parent of a student from the school. She has recently returned from a vacation.

Field trips are a big part of our programming at Lawrence Heights. So far this year classes have gone to the library and are scheduled to visit YTV, CityTV and Nortel. Today the teacher of our behaviour program returns from a visit to Jungle Cat World. They have a terrific visit and arrange for an exhibit of the jungle cats to come to our school.

The *Toronto Star* journalist visits again to take some pictures and do some more interviews. The story is to appear in the Greater Toronto section on Saturday, October 2.

SEPTEMBER 29

During my classroom visits today I take in a math lesson in the computer lab. The students are thoroughly engaged in their math lesson which is provided by the Learning Equation computer program. The math lessons average ninety minutes of work, plus additional practice. The pedagogical model is comprised of seven modules that engage the student first in exploring an application of the math concept of the lesson, then teach, demonstrate and summarize the concept, then provide practice and testing. The program is fully interactive, user friendly and visually appealing, so the students love it.

A parent calls to report her concern about a student in her daughter's class having head lice. A staff member checks it out after calling the student's home and confirms the concern. We send the student home and send a letter to the parents of the students in the class.

I send a memo off to our grade convenors asking them, now that we have completed the assessments on our students, what are the next steps: what are we doing to provide programming to meet their individual needs? How will we help students who are below grade level in numeracy and literacy, and those who need to be further challenged?

SEPTEMBER 30

Upon my arrival this morning at 7:40 I am greeted by a group of girls from the choir who would like to sing a song. They do a fine job and it is a great way for me to start my day.

Shortly after, another student drops by to ask for some help with his speech. He is running for president in the student elections. I encourage him to omit all the references he makes in the speech to how good looking he is.

In the mail today I receive a *SciencePower* textbook. The publishers have sent out the text to students and staff of our school who were involved with field testing the book.

Tonight is the barbecue and although the weather isn't great we are still hoping for a good turnout.

OCTOBER 1

Boys basketball practice starts today. A few students are disappointed that they can't try out because they don't have all "yes" on their progress report. We have outlined criteria for sport participation at our school through our Balancing Academics, Sports and Education program (B.A.S.E.).

Sports are a very important part of the lives of our students. It is an

Balancing Academics, Sports and Education

Mission Statement
We recognize sports in our society as an activity that may provide opportunities for character building and may have a critical effect in socializing youth. Through participation in sports one learns not only how to play a specific sport, but also how to play the game of life.

Research has resulted in consistent findings that participation in athletics increases educational aspirations (Spence 1999). This increase in educational aspirations has been attributed to two major theories:

- Personal contact hypothesis states that students gain positive contacts with peers and staff through sports;
- Athletic involvement helps students achieve academic success. This argument asserts that sports improve students' self-concept, thereby leading them to develop higher aspirations for themselves.

Criteria
The expectations for students participating in sports at Lawrence Heights for the 1999–2000 school year are that students must:

- Have all "yes" on their progress report
- Have a signed contract with their parent/guardian's signature
- Be consistently meeting or exceeding academic/behaviour expectations
- Must attend study hall sessions implemented by the coaches.

area in which they can excel and be recognized. Sports motivate them and provide an emotional outlet. But does the pursuit of sporting success somehow diminish academic excellence?

When you visit a high school, what is the first thing that you see? James Coleman's (1987) work stands as a key source on the subject. He studied ten different high schools to determine the impact of a variety of influences on the educational performance of teenagers. He studied the adolescent culture, and he began his argument with the contention that all students seek status, respect and recognition in the eyes of their peers and their teachers.

He found the two main sources of recognition are athletics and academics, with athletics being more widely valued. He found that the most talented athletes tend to be drawn into the pursuit of athletic excellence. However, potentially excellent scholars are not drawn into

A student proudly displays B.A.S.E. painting on the lockers

scholarship because the status to be gained is less.

At Lawrence Heights there is no doubt that if you want status, sport participation is a way of getting it. The recognition gained by playing on the school basketball team is quite extraordinary. Basketball more than any other sport continues to be seen as a way out and a way to realize your dreams.

As a matter of fact the status of successful athletes has resulted in their becoming the primary role models among Black youth. This success often operates in concert with peer group pressure among students to under-perform academically. If you go into any elementary school I'm sure you'll find that somewhere near 90 percent of all young Black males want to be a professional athlete when they grow up. It becomes a problem when educators start believing that Black kids are simply not able or interested in succeeding academically and that sports is their best shot.

There is nothing wrong with having goals, but realistically less than 1 percent of them will ever see that goal achieved. What happens to all the rest? Aspiring "I wanna be like Mike" kids, spend countless hours mastering their dribbling and shooting skills with little thought to their future when their sports days are done. They will be helping the great ones become even greater. And when they realize the dream won't come true for them, they become an entire generation of could-have-beens. They spend so much time preparing to be great athletes that in many cases their studies have suffered.

We as a society ask for this, we even set aside a major segment of our daily newspaper and television programming to highlight athletic achievement. We don't do that for science fair winners. Nor do we see college scouts visiting inner-city school math classes. The real social champions in our society are not the ones who run with an idea, but the ones who run with a ball.

My interest in this area stems from my own sporting background and the realization of the significant role sport has played in my life. Sport has helped me organize my sense of self and my understanding of the world, and it is the way I spend much of my leisure time. In my experience, sports function as a source of discipline and self-esteem, qualities that contribute to life long success.

My interest in this area is also a result of my daily interactions with youth, and Black youth specifically, as a coach, educator and friend. Many of these youth have articulated a desire to pursue a professional sports career above all else. Many of these students have revealed that they are recognized as outstanding participants but their academic involvement is viewed suspiciously. This prevailing attitude cannot be attributed solely to the games participants nor to the schools. It is a reflection of society in general.

The barbecue was a huge success: great music (a band with staff and students), great people (staff, students, parents and community members), and great food (tasty home burgers). We are all on a high today.

The situation with Mandy reaches a crisis point today when she claims to be hearing voices that are telling her to stab and kill anyone who bothers her. We call Children's Aid and they direct us to take her to the hospital to be assessed by a psychiatrist. Tom returns only to say that after being assessed the doctor says she is okay and not to worry! We explain our concerns to her father who comes to pick her up. He seems to be more interested in his work schedule for the day. He is obviously at the end of the line with his daughter and still thinks sending her to Jamaica is the answer.

A student returns to the school after a lengthy vacation in Bangladesh and brings a beautiful piece of art for the school.

I am touched by a grandfather (not biological) who has demonstrated a keen interest in two of our students. He routinely pops in to give them lunch money or just to say "hi." Every time the kids see him their eyes light up and they come running to greet him.

Today, we have our first student of the month assembly. We start every recognition assembly with the Kool and the Gang tune "Celebration." Students are recognized and celebrated in front of their peers and are given a medal of learning.

It is always great to see some of our former students drop by. They always tell us how much they miss the school and how they wish they were still attending. A grade 10 student drops by; he is looking particularly sharp. He asks a teacher for a ride to his first job interview.

OCTOBER 4

I start my morning at the YMCA gym, where I work out, and I am stopped by a number of the members who congratulate me on the terrific article in the *Toronto Star*. One member tells me he had his kids read the article because he thought it was so positive. Another promises to give our school some complementary tickets to sporting events. I also receive a number of calls and e-mails from colleagues who are all enthusiastic about the article. Students and staff are feeling good about the positive exposure of our school. At home our phone rings off the hook. What a great feeling—this is something that will be shared by the students, staff, community and parents of Lawrence Heights for quite some time.

A parent drops by to discuss her son. We are really concerned that Malik is starting his last year here on the wrong track. He is a capable student but picks and chooses when he is going to produce. We talk to him about high school and the need for him to change his nonchalant attitude. His mother has always been a strong advocate for him, but I sense she is losing her patience. She promises to sign her son up for a tutoring program run by the Jamaican Canadian Association.

Sandy and Steve's parent visits this morning. I outline the plan of action. Sandy tries to pull me into a discussion about other students and how they were consequenced. I have no part of that discussion and refocus on the issue—her disrespectful attitude! The meeting ends on an emotional note as Sandy's mother is very upset. She makes it very clear that she is fed up.

This week at grade assemblies we will talk about what makes a great student. We will talk about how success in any course of study is more often the result of good organization than of individual brilliance. Only through good organization and careful management of time, will a student be successful. Successful students demonstrate a combination of successful attitudes and behaviours. Successful students get involved in their studies, accept responsibility for their own education and are active participants in their education. Responsibility means control. It's the difference between leading and being led. Students' own efforts control their grade. They can sit there, act bored, daydream, fool around or sleep. Or they can actively listen, think, question and take good notes.

Successful students have educational goals. Students need to ask themselves these questions: What am I doing here? Is there somewhere else I'd rather be? What does my presence at school mean to me? Answers to these questions represent the most important factors in a child's success as a student. If a child's educational goals are truly her or his own, and not someone else's, these goals will motivate the child to adopt a positive academic attitude.

Successful students ask questions. In addition to securing knowledge, they seek information. Asking questions has at least two other extremely important benefits. The process helps students pay attention to their teacher and helps their teacher pay attention to the student. There are no foolish questions, only foolish silence. Asking and talking about the material is a sure way of learning the material. The question of what leads to success has been explored by John H. Williams in his work entitled, "What Makes a Great Student? Clarifying Grade Expectations" (1993). It's your choice.

Terri chairs a new teachers meeting that I drop in on. The meeting gives first and second year teachers at the school the opportunity to share best practices and ask any questions about policies, procedures and curriculum.

OCTOBER 5

We get off to a rocky start this morning. A grade 6 student tells us he is being harassed by two grade 8 students. After investigating the situation we find that all involved are partially responsible. Some provoked and some acted irresponsibly. It is not the way we want to start our day. It is disappointing because we spend so much time talking about respect. The fact that this happened off of school property just doesn't matter. Every time students put on their uniforms they are accountable to the school.

The phone calls are still coming in about the *Toronto Star* article. In fact one school even asked for a copy of the progress report that was mentioned in the article. We gladly fax it off. The Toronto Raptors called and offered us tickets to upcoming games. A late afternoon call from a former student of Lawrence Heights (she attended ten years ago) is uplifting. She thought the article was about a private school and is amazed with the changes we have made.

We are very fortunate to have established a partnership with Victoria College of the University of Toronto. Long before I arrived here there have been outstanding students from Victoria College who come in and volunteer their services. Last year they were actively involved in our math, science and technology clubs and also were involved in spelling bees and public speaking. Today we have a group of twelve from Victoria College at the school who are interested in gaining some practical experience. We look forward to working with them and providing a supportive environment in which they can grow and learn.

OCTOBER 6

I meet with Tika, a student who is feeling down and out. Her father has threatened to send her back to Ghana if she doesn't do better in school. Thus far she hasn't had a good start to the school year. She seems to be preoccupied with boys and clothes; academics is not her top priority. She is currently in the L.E.A.P. class, but continually comes with a less than stellar attitude. I encourage her to take her academics more seriously and ask her what I can do to help.

We have been awaiting the arrival of our test scores from the Education Quality and Accountability Office (EQAO). They arrive this morning. Last year during the month of May, all grade 3 and 6 students across the province were involved in testing administered by the EQAO. The testing included reading, writing and mathematics.

In an effort to enrich curriculum to the fullest extent possible and to evaluate students more fairly, there is a move to replace standardized tests with performance-based assessments. Such assessments stress the problem-solving skills that schools should be teaching, make good diagnostic instruments and are much better at eliciting the potential of students.

The best way to discover how students think or to diagnose where they are having difficulties in learning—which, aside from accountability, is the main reason for testing—is to give them as much of a range of options as possible to express themselves fully (Archbald and Newmann 1988). It is also important to assess their learning in its natural context, as they make active use of a particular skill (Gardner, in press).

While traditional standardized tests assume that a multiple choice question about possible grammatical solutions to an incorrect sentence can indicate a student's writing skills, performance-based assessments simply sample the student's writing itself. While traditional tests are scored on the basis of objective notions of right and wrong answers, performance-based assessments entail clear human judgements. Whereas most standardized tests measure only discrete linguistic and number skills, assessments in context can assess a far wider range of competencies (Gardner, in press). Like life, where most of the important problems faced are open ended and complex, performance-based assessments require that each student demonstrates mastery in a personal and more integrated way (Archbald and Newmann 1988). Also in contrast to standardized tests, which have predictive validity, performance assessments have "ecological validity"(that is, students perform as they will have to in life.

My concern with the standardized tests is that they don't necessarily take into account all the other variables that can have an effect on schooling. But, more importantly, they don't measure the growth of the students' abilities throughout the year. If a student is given an overall level 3 standing (provincial standard) in math, there is nothing to indicate where he or she started. What if the student was a level 1 and worked so hard or was a part of an innovative program to help increase her or his competency in a particular area?

I say this only because I believe that it is not only where you are at that is important, but also where you are coming from. At our school I know our students and staff work extremely hard to produce the results that we have received, but good, bad or indifferent, these don't tell the whole story.

Proponents of standardized tests often wrap themselves in the language of high standards. I just don't think that is the issue; no educator or parent that I know advocates for low standards. The issue is what we mean by higher standards, and how we can reach those standards. By and large, calls for more standardized tests come from politicians eager to appear serious about school reform—such is the case with our present government in Ontario. But the tests offer little if any evidence that links increased testing to improved teaching and learning. Similarly, testing advocates pay little attention to the need for smaller class sizes, improved teacher education, more time for teacher planning and collaboration, and ensuring that all schools receive adequate and equitable resources to support student achievement.

While doing my classroom visits today I talk to convenors about a potential problem around snack provision. It seems a staff member has excluded her class from the snack break because of homework incompletion. I ask convenors to discuss that philosophy, which I am opposed to. No student should be denied the snack provision, plain and simple. Taking away the snack for not doing homework is not a logical consequence.

It is nice at the end of the day to receive a call from the music coordinator about our students who are attending a workshop. She says our students were terrific and we should be very proud. They were focused, productive and demonstrated a lot of talent, even outperforming some of the high school students in attendance.

We have our first curriculum night this evening for grade 8 students and parents. About one-third of the parents show up. We still need to do more to get parents out for important events like this. Our home high school staff speak about their high school and the programs they offer, then staff meet with parents of students in their class.

OCTOBER 8

Today gets off to a rocky start when a couple of male students square off outside. The dispute is over money. One student lent another student some money and wants it back today. Luckily, a staff member is on duty and is able to defuse the situation real quick. One of the students involved is Steve. Someone that we continue to worry about. His mother has now said if anything happens at school don't call her, call the police.

Today our student council candidates present their speeches to the school. It is terrific to see such a diverse group talk about their accomplishments and leadership potential. We only have one male running for office, but all the candidates are outstanding. The student body is reminded that this not a popularity contest; student council requires students to be responsible and demonstrate leadership potential.

OCTOBER 13

I am inspired by a three-hour meeting with our family of schools superintendent. She is thoughtful and insightful in her analysis of our school plan and asks the kinds of questions that challenge me as a leader. We share philosophies and strategies and just brainstorm about how to make a difference in the lives of our students. Her experience with her own children gives her a unique and thought provoking perspective.

The role of the superintendent has become more complex and demanding. She is responsible for twenty schools. She deals with educational reform, new legislation, collective bargaining and rapid changes in social and cultural conditions, such as multilingual classrooms. All of these changes have made educational leadership a much different task from how it was previously conceived and practised. Today's leaders must mobilize resources to build a culture that is committed to learning. Parents want assurances that the changes are being implemented at a pace that their children and the teachers can handle.

Our staff meeting today deals mainly with special education. We revisit modification strategies for special program students. This has become an issue particularly in light of the stance we have taken with progress reports. Students and parents know that in order to participate in any extracurricular activities students must have all the "yes" boxes checked on their report. If a special education student receives a "no" and the program was not modified, this creates a lot of difficulties. Modification strategies are provided by Kirk, our head of special education.

A late night phone call from Danny, a former student, brings good news. He was charged last year for his role in an assault. The case has been ongoing since then and required myself and another teacher to testify on his behalf in court and to be a supervisor for his release. He has now been found not guilty and can go about leading a productive life. The whole situation caused so much aggravation, particularly for his mother, as the conditions for his release required constant supervision. He couldn't even ride the bus by himself. I am glad it is over.

Responding to a student's concern, Tom visits a man in the community who is alleged to be following students from our school. The conversation doesn't seem to make an impact on the man as he laughs throughout the teacher's conversation with him. We call the police and put the students and the school's community on alert.

OCTOBER 14

An early morning call from a colleague is saddening. They had a situation at their school that got out of control. Fire alarms were being pulled throughout the day and students were not following appropriate procedures. The situation reached a boiling point when a firefighter and some students got into an altercation.

Another successful curriculum night hosted by our grade 7 team. A satisfactory turnout of parents, but all too often it ends up being a session where we are preaching to the converted. The challenge at this school is to reach some of the parents who have traditionally stayed away for various reasons.

Next week we will have our first parent council meeting and the same kind of problems exist in terms of trying to get the parents out. One of our more creative solutions was to run a Playstation (video games) tournament, but in order to participate students needed to bring their parent to the council meeting. That was a huge success.

OCTOBER 18

Our school trip to YTV's *Uh Oh* show was a tremendous success. Students and staff come back on a real high. If you've never seen the show you have to take it in, it is so much fun for the students—they absolutely love it. The prizes that the students win are the best (such as a keyboard or snowboard) and every student gets a T-shirt and a bag of goodies to take home.

We did however have some difficulty with the selection of students who could attend the show. As with all extracurricular activities, students needed to have all the "yes" boxes on their progress reports checked to attend. As a result there were quite a few disappointed students, and even a few parents called. We did however stick to our guns and not allow students with a "no" to attend. I think that sends out a strong message to all our students.

Our Boys to Men program is up and running. We have now been on two trips, one to an Argonaut game and the other to the University of Toronto open house. The participants just love the opportunity to extend the school day on a Friday or a weekend get together.

We have now sent three students home this year for racist comments. We try to follow that up with some counselling from our guidance department and make it a part of a staff advisor program. Today a student is sent home for telling a Muslim student to "get that piece of garbage off of her head." The student is obviously upset over the comment. We contact both parents to let them know what has happened and the consequences for that kind of behaviour. Incidents like this remind us that anti-racist education is a pedagogy and not an add-on. Last year the whole staff participated in a three-day professional development session around equity and anti-racist education, so we are able to deal with these kind of issues effectively. An anti-racist reading is sent to staff (see Appendix C).

The focus of today's assembly is fundraising. We are going to be selling chocolates this year, but it is important that we discuss the safety issues and the time frame with which we will be working. Students are always motivated and interested in fundraising for the school. We give out great prizes to those students who have sold the most chocolates.

Anytime we have the whole school together we also take the opportu-

Boys to Men

Objectives
The objective of the Boys to Men program is to provide a look at the reality that many at-risk students may face. Students need to know that dropping out of the academic culture of school may lead to serious consequences. They may have to face the harsh, uncompromising job market with inadequate credentials and job skills; young dropouts have to settle for a lifetime of unskilled wage labour, or even no job.

Boys to Men was created with this message in mind. We seek to convey a very important message to at-risk youth in an attempt to override aspects of the cultural environment that exist outside of the school. After the family, the school stands as the most important cultural institution contributing to the education and socialization of youth. We have these youth in our care for six hours, five days a week, ten months of the year. Thus we can foster positive growth and development.

Boys to Men includes the following ideals:

Role models
Many at-risk male students suffer from a lack of appropriate male models in their neighbourhoods and at home, and they have few men with whom to bond. Thus the program offers positive images of male adulthood through male teachers, mentors, advocates and other role models.

Transition to manhood
The assumption is that boys from fatherless homes may have difficulty moving toward manhood and may participate in gangs as a spontaneous form of initiation. Therefore, the use of initiation rites to direct and dignify the transition from boyhood to manhood is necessary. These initiation rites include acquiring new knowledge, rules of conduct, setting goals and providing community service.

Identity/Self-Esteem
The assumption here is that the self-esteem of at-risk male students is battered by the pervasive negative images of people like themselves on the streets, in schools and in the media. Because the values and self-discipline needed for achievement are thought to be absent in much of an at-risk student's life, the program attempts to develop a system of values and social skills that will

facilitate success in the school and work world. At the same time, Boys to Men has strict attendance rules, gives assistance with school work, helps students with non-violent conflict resolution and tries to develop responsible sexual norms. In all this, the hope is to instill new behaviours that will lead to greater ease with and respect from adults both in school and in the work world.

Safe Haven
Finally, and underlying all the components of the program, is the conviction that many at-risk males need an environment that shelters them from, and is a positive alternative to, their subcultures. Thus the program often protects students from the street by extending the school day and providing healthy, alternative routes for expressing male values and behaviour.

The Boys to Men program is an effort to develop new and creative models that are intrinsic to the educative process that is aimed at preventing the development of negative attitudes toward life and academic achievement.

nity to discuss the good, the bad and the ugly at Lawrence Heights. We always try to start with the positive and there continues to be a lot of good at Lawrence, like the recent student council elections, the upcoming dance, recent trips to CityTV, YTV, the opening of the gamesroom and the upcoming trip to a Raptor basketball game.

The bad includes homework completion, which is still an area of concern. Also certain students show a lack of attitude and gratitude, particularly around the snack program. The other day when the snack was bananas, numerous peels were found all over the school.

The ugly was a student hanging up on me. When she asked to go to YTV, I asked about her progress report and she hung up on me. Another student threatened that if he didn't get to go to YTV he wouldn't do any work for the rest of the year. Lastly, a student left his clothes in the change room and someone put his pants in the toilet and put pop in his shoes.

Once again the message is one of accountability. Students are accountable for their behaviour and their commitment to learning. As a staff we will support and encourage students, but they must meet us half way.

OCTOBER 19

Today we started our transition program for our grade 5 students. We visit our feeder schools, invite the students and their parents to our school and describe our philosophy.

Today's visit was a huge success. The grade 6 ambassadors who accompanied me on the visit did an outstanding job articulating what Lawrence Heights is all about.

What is Racism?

Racism is the mistreatment of a group of people on the basis of race, colour, religion, national origin, place of origin or ancestry. The term racism may also denote a blind and unreasoning hatred, envy or prejudice.

Some expressions of racism are obvious, such as name calling, graffiti, intimidation or physical violence. Racial and ethnic slurs or so-called jokes are other examples of obvious racial discrimination. Unfortunately, they are often ignored because people do not know how to deal with them.

At Lawrence we believe that racism poisons the atmosphere of trust that we need in order for all students to feel valued and respected. Racist jokes and racial discrimination leave their victims feeling helpless and fearful. We frequently remind everyone in the building that they have a responsibility to speak out against racism. Not doing so may be interpreted as tacit approval of discrimination.

Some of the things we have done at Lawrence, and are working toward, are:

- Objecting to racist jokes and insults
- Inviting guests to speak on racism and human rights
- Participating in activities marking the International Day for the Elimination of Racial Discrimination every March 21
- Exploring ways in which community organizations and the school can work together to promote positive race relations
- Organizing a poster or essay contest
- Showing films on prejudice, stereotyping, discrimination and racism
- Examining the contents of television, film, radio and newspapers
- Finding out about human rights organizations in our area and what role they play
- Ongoing professional development for staff
- Development of a school policy on race relations and the formation of a race relations committee.

OCTOBER 20

What a challenging day! It is days like today that make me wonder if our message is falling on deaf ears. Issues of respect are the order of the day. A handful of students refuse to meet the expectations of the school. For the most part they are repeat offenders, the ones who just don't get it. They continue to be a powerful force in the school. We suspend some and

Grade 6.

For many older students those words bring back thoughts of their first few months at a middle school. During this time they were learning to find their way around the school, figuring out how to use their lockers, buying their lunch, being exposed to different teaching styles and timetables, making new friends, learning and discovering new ideas and knowledge.

Lawrence Heights is working to improve these grade 6 memories for today's students through the following areas of focus:

Professional Dialogue
The lines of communication between grade 5 sending teachers and grade 6 receiving teachers are open. This allows teachers to discuss individual student needs, strategies, areas of strengths and concerns.

Parent Contact and Involvement
This process introduces parents and students to school related factors, such as policies and practices within the school. Lawrence Heights is an effective school with the following components:
Focus, mission, vision
High academic expectations
Collaboration
Participation, connectedness, sense of belonging, positive school climate
Relevance, integration
Monitoring, reinforcement and feedback

Lawrence Heights has an open door policy and welcomes parental input and involvement, and will be extending an invitation to parents to participate in our School Council.

Student Learning Activities
At the centre of the transition process is the student. As part of our program students will visit the school and be engaged in school activities.

schedule meetings with parents for others. We are going to have to look to alternative programs I would suspect for others. It is non-stop throughout the day.

It continues into the evening when three parents came by to discuss their daughters' perceptions of preferential treatment by staff. I think everyone walked away realizing the need to reflect on how we are interacting with one another.

The day ends with yet another successful curriculum night, this one hosted by the grade 6 team. It is by far our best turnout, which is usually the way it is at middle schools. Grade 6 students are always eager and willing to bring their parents out to events like this. Unfortunately, by the time they get to grade 7 and 8 the interest tends to wane a bit. Our challenge as educators is to keep that momentum going throughout the schooling process.

We certainly receive a lot of positive feedback from the parents and support for our firm but fair approach. We emphasize that the focus will continue to be on academics.

OCTOBER 21

Our in-school professional development program begins today. Amber, a staff member with a superior knowledge of the Adolescent Literacy Project and who is a leader in the school, will visit every grade team meeting to discuss the implementation, modelling and expectation of evidence of the program in every classroom.

We are fortunate to have a number of exceptional teachers at our school who are able to deliver meaningful professional development sessions with strategies that can be used in the classroom immediately. Earlier in the year we did a session on computers in the classroom, which was done by Evan, our head of science and technology, and a staff member.

It is exciting to be working with the equity coordinator for our school region on a proposal that would see my new book, *The Skin I'm In: Racism, Sport and Education,* be used as a point of discussion with physical education teachers and administrators. The book explores the relationship between athletic participation by Black male students and their academic and career aspirations.

With thirty parents turning out for our first school council meeting we are feeling it is a success. We invited guest speaker Richard Mathieu, a financial planner with Primerica, to do a presentation on the Registered Education Savings Plans. It was an informative presentation that really emphasized the need to think beyond grade 12 to ensure a quality of life that will allow for choices in the future.

There is a lot of disappointment today after the third progress report of the year is given out. A lot of students fly off the handle and make some strong statements. Some even play the race card, citing this as the reason for their failure. The scheduled trip to Detroit with our choir is certainly in jeopardy. I think the best thing to do is to step back and think about things over the weekend. Everyone's emotions are running high right now.

OCTOBER 25

Emotions are still running high, but I address the issues through a school-wide assembly. Before doing so I investigate thoroughly the allegations that are being made. What it comes down to is that some students want something for nothing. They continue to think that just showing up every day and not being disruptive means they are learning. Imagine a student throwing a temper tantrum because she got a "no" on her progress report for choosing not to submit two out of their three language arts assignments? Or students complaining even though they were given more than one opportunity to pass an open book test? This has nothing to do with race, this is about expectations that these students are not meeting.

I reiterate the same message to the student body—winning starts with beginning. You must begin to accept responsibility for your actions. You choose to win or lose. The message will not change, but your actions must. Staff and students know I am ticked. I walk out of the assembly leaving everyone wondering where I've gone. I am touched several times throughout the day when students and staff want to know if I am okay. This is tough love.

OCTOBER 26

Steve and Sandy are acting up again. This is after they have been relatively quiet. Sandy refuses to write a test and ends up ripping it in two and throwing it. She scribbles all over another assignment and says she is not doing it. Steve tells one of our assistants to "fuck off." The whole building pretty much has to come to a stop because he is so loud and out of order. Both will certainly be consequenced for their actions.

A confrontation in the choir with a sister of one of our students is quickly defused by a staff member. It could have been dangerous. The older sister tells me she is sick and tired of Freda, a student at the school, who continues to bother her sister Louise. Louise comes home every day complaining and doesn't want to come to school. So the older sister decided to take matters into her own hands and confront those she suspected were troubling her sister. Well, when she confronted the students Freda called her a fucking bitch. That comment put her over the deep end and she went after Freda. Luckily, a staff member was there to intervene.

Too many students return late after lunch today. Thus far this year we have made dramatic improvements around lates, but today is not good. What drives me crazy is their excuse is they were in line at Kentucky Fried Chicken for "Tooney Tuesday"!

One hundred students have the opportunity to attend a Raptor game this evening and it is magical. For many of the students it is their first time in the Air Canada Centre. It is a great evening for all those students who earned the privilege through their progress reports.

OCTOBER 27

My morning starts with a meeting at Xerox. Our former superintendent hosts the event. It is extremely exciting because of the potential of the latest Xerox technology, DocuShare, which has some amazing capabilities. We are asked to go back to our school and collect data to determine the economic feasibility of DocuShare.

Today we hold our first dance and there are a lot of tears being shed by students who are not able to attend because of their progress reports. Part of the difficulty is that apparently a student who had four "no" boxes checked went to the Raptor game last night. We have to investigate further but he played one teacher against another by saying that the other said it was okay. This has resulted in a number of students crying foul.

NOVEMBER 1

The first school day after Halloween always seems to be a difficult one. Students are more energized than usual today, probably because of the candy.

A parent drops by in the morning and is concerned for her daughter's safety. Apparently a group of students from the school went to her house and were intimidating her and her daughter. The situation could have been explosive but luckily it didn't end up that way. The family is new to the neighbourhood and the parent is afraid of what might happen. Now, she also has a role in this because she told the students to stay away from her daughter or she would take care of them herself. As you can imagine this got the students all fired up and they threatened to involve their parents and friends. I speak to all involved and they seem to understand the seriousness of the situation. The alleged victim in this situation also has a role as she has been provoking the students.

Recently, there was a stabbing in a Montreal school around the latest Pokemon craze. So when a father of a student at our school shows up and is concerned that someone went into his son's knapsack and stole his Pokemon cards the investigation began. It will continue until this is resolved.

A terrific day for field trips at our school. Students go to the zoo and Canadian Airlines and come back as happy as can be.

Since the article in the *Toronto Star* I have had numerous requests to do some motivational speaking and presentations. I recently did a presentation for IBM and was an inspirational speaker for the Martin Kruze Forum. Martin was the individual who disclosed sexual abuse that he suffered down at Maple Leaf Gardens.

We receive the EQAO results for our school and we are below the provincial standards in all three areas. For reading 41 percent of our students are at level 3 and 4 (out of four levels), 44 percent for writing and

46 percent for mathematics. Most importantly the results allow us to examine what we are doing at the school to address the gaps in learning.

NOVEMBER 2

Jungle Cat World visits our school today and what a morning it is. They provide a unique interactive approach to endangered species education. Throughout the presentation they focus on wildlife from all corners of the globe and give the students the opportunity to meet some of the special guests that include a wolf, a baby jaguar and a fourteen-foot python. Everyone enjoys the presentation, which is both informative and entertaining.

We have started doing classroom visits to observe teachers and so far so good. I have always been impressed with the calibre of teachers at this school. They work really hard and are dedicated and professional educators. As administrators in the school we really see ourselves as providing a support mechanism for the staff. Classroom observations and evaluations give us a chance to see evidence of the great work the staff are doing and to make recommendations as to how they can improve. Being a lifelong learner and continuous improvement are emphasized. We are all accountable, therefore evidence of planning, preparation, assessment, tracking, evaluation and school-wide initiatives (such as implementation of First Steps or the Adolescent Reading Project) are expected.

I also expect to see instructional groups formed in the classroom to fit students' academic and affective needs. For example, when introducing new concepts and skills, whole group instruction, actively led by the teacher, is preferable. The use of heterogeneous cooperative learning groups, structured so that there are both group rewards and individual accountability, is encouraged.

We also expect to see evidence of high expectations for classroom behaviour and measures that are applied consistently and equitably. Procedures should be carried out quickly and be clearly linked to students' inappropriate behaviour. Teachers should also reinforce positive social behaviours.

Teachers are expected to make use of effective questioning techniques that are used to develop basic and higher level skills, and to check students' understanding and stimulate their thinking. Lastly, we expect students will routinely receive feedback and reinforcement regarding their learning progress. Praise and other verbal reinforcements should be provided for correct answers and for participation and progress in relation to past performance.

Today's student of the month assembly is a first for us because it is done using a PowerPoint presentation. Students set it up and operate it very successful. I have been disappointed in previous assemblies with the lack of recognition students receive from their peers. In my mind these students should receive a rousing ovation. They have worked hard and deserve our respect. A couple of days before the assembly I sent a note to all staff indicating the assembly would come to a stop if students weren't applauded appropriately. The assembly is a success.

NOVEMBER 8

I return to school today after being away with the choir on a tour of Southern Ontario. The whole trip was absolute MAGIC! Students and staff had an amazing time performing and interacting with students from Kitchener, Windsor and Detroit. The schools we visited were similar to ours and were inspiring for me as an educator to learn from.

We also visited the Motown Museum, which was fitting since our performance is called "A Slice of Motown." We got to meet and perform for some of the legends of Motown, including Beans Bowles, a member of the Marvellettes, and Berry Gordy's sister.

Choir on their tour of Southern Ontario

We have an informative professional development session that focusses on our First Steps training, which addresses student writing. A development continuum has been prepared to assist teachers who are assessing students' writing and helping the students to improve it. The continuum has four levels and key indicators at each level. The majority of our staff assessed themselves to be at level three, which is the application phase. At this stage teachers improve the students' writing by implementing the First Steps philosophy and strategies on a daily basis.

There continues to be concern around the progress reports. We are still experiencing growing pains around the initiative. Most of the concerns are around equity and consistency from staff. We are going to continue to discuss the program and modify it where necessary. I have, however, made it very clear that we will not abandon the progress reports.

NOVEMBER 9

Today, I had the opportunity to be part of the interview team for principals in Toronto. I still remember hearing that you are only a true leader when you prepare others to take over for you. It was a terrific experience to be a part of the process that will secure the leadership for our board. I worked with and learned from a principal and a superintendent who brought their expertise and knowledge to the table.

NOVEMBER 10

A touching and memorable Remembrance Day assembly is the highlight of the day. Our grade 8 students put on a terrific display of reading, writing, drama, song and dance. We have such a talented student body.

Our first home game of the basketball season is today. We really try to make it an event. Students know that they have to have all "yes" on their progress reports to attend and they have to sign a spectator agreement form to get in.

The team gets off to a great start, which is terrific because a couple of our key players have not met the academic expectations of the school. They were convinced the team couldn't win without them and that we would give in and let them play. I don't think so.

NOVEMBER 12

We never do it enough, but today we make time to celebrate our staff. A morning breakfast of appreciation is our way of saying "thank you" to the staff for all they do to make Lawrence Heights a great school. I am absolutely convinced that this staff is second to none in terms of their commitment to making a difference. Long hours and a passion to see our students succeed are the driving forces at our school.

A difficult situation arises today when a supply teacher who has had difficulty here in the past shows up to supply. About a year and half ago I

Spectator Agreement

To be a spectator at a Lawrence Heights sporting event, I recognize that I am a representative of the school and will not do anything to harm the reputation of the school. Therefore, I will conduct myself in a way that meets the expectations of the Lawrence Heights Code of Behaviour.

I agree to the following expectations:

- Detentions and extra help come first
- I must leave the building promptly after the game
- There are no in/out privileges during the game
- I understand, due to space limitations, I may not gain admittance to the event
- Failure to comply with the above expectations will result in a loss of my spectator privileges.

had a conversation with this teacher and strongly encouraged her not to return. There have been numerous issues brought to my attention by staff and students concerning this supply teacher. I speak to her again today and remind her that I will have no choice but to conduct an evaluation of her teaching the next time she accepts a job at our school. That evaluation may affect her employment possibilities and that is somewhere we don't want to go.

NOVEMBER 15

A busy day at Lawrence Heights. Two grade 6 classes go to the Hobberlin Museum. This hands-on teaching facility illustrates the scientific principles of how the earth works using hundreds of actual fossils and recent animal specimens, thousands of rocks and minerals, and many space related materials.

Unfortunately, before the trip has ended Yolanda has to be escorted back to the school because of her rude behaviour. We talk so much about students being ambassadors for the school every time they leave the school. Her teacher is very disappointed and by the look on his face he means business. In all likelihood this is her last trip of the year.

Amber, our grade 8 convenor, has organized a terrific learning experience for our grade 8 students. She has invited a drama production to the school that focuses on the issues faced by grade 9 students. We also invited other middle schools to the performance and have two classes from Brookview join us. The performance is funny and engaging and offers a unique perspective. The students and staff enjoy the afternoon.

Tom found the time to rustle up four tickets to see Motown recording artist Brian McKnight perform on the Mike Bullard Show, and tickets for Destiny's Child. We decide to raffle off the tickets because of the huge amount of interest.

Our Gifted Readers Club make my day when they invite me to be a guest author at their meeting. I speak about my new book, *The Skin I'm In*, and share some of my experiences. The students are responsive and interested. What a great way to end the day!

NOVEMBER 16

A visit to our school from our superintendent, Karen Forbes, and executive officer, Mary Low, is the highlight of the day. It is a great opportunity for us to showcase the great things that we are doing at the school. They are greeted by our student ambassadors and are given a tour of the school. Some of the key stops are the library and the terrific program that we are offering; the computer lab, where students are working on the Learning Equation; and the drama room where the choir is rehearsing for an upcoming performance on CityTV.

Our visitors stop in on every classroom to meet and greet staff and students. It is a great day for us. They like what they see: programs and activities that reflect the efforts of a dedicated staff. I feel good for the staff—they deserve to be recognized.

In the afternoon I do a presentation at York University to a group of third year education students in teachers' college. I spend most of my time sharing my philosophy on education and the philosophy of our school. The students ask some great questions and share some of their insights on the education system as they embark on a career in teaching. I conclude the presentation by showing the Lawrence Heights promo video, which they enjoy, and by reminding them that passion and the belief that all children can learn are necessary for their future success.

NOVEMBER 17

The African Canadian Cultural Club starts up today. It provides students with the opportunity to study the positive contributions of people of African ancestry.

The first and second year teachers' meeting chaired by Terri continues to provide new teachers to the school with the opportunity to share best practices. Today a detailed science lesson is shared complete with resources and tracking sheets. Also shared is an independent reading program called D.E.A.R. (Drop Everything and Read).

The police pay a visit to the school to inquire about a fight that took place off school property. The parents of one of the students involved called the police. At our end the students are counselled and suspended. While the police are here we take the opportunity to discuss with them our concern about Steve, who is quickly becoming a menace to the community. A couple of hours later they make some follow-up calls to the child's parent and outline some options for courses of action.

NOVEMBER 19

This morning I meet with my Project Pride group to discuss the program. I will be mentoring seven students and will have daily contact with them and weekly phone contact with their parents. This is in an effort to help some of our students be more responsible for their actions and to achieve academically. Today, we have breakfast and discuss academic aspirations.

I am shocked to return to the school and find that our secretary was at our local bank making a deposit when the bank was robbed. She was at the clerk's desk when this happened and was a short distance from a pointed gun—a traumatic experience for anyone. Luckily, no one was injured, but she is understandably a little shaken up. We advise her to go home for the afternoon.

The senseless beating death of Toronto District School Board student Matti Baranovski, who was swarmed two blocks from his home after being confronted by a group of up to twelve masked thugs, has certainly made

Students in my Project Pride Group

us all reflect on the safety of our students. At Lawrence Heights we process the situation through our school assemblies and through individual classes. Students talk about it and ask questions, but their main concern is that no one has been arrested. Students are remarkably sympathetic and empathetic but are confused as to why someone would do something so stupid.

NOVEMBER 20

I spend most of my Saturday fundraising with the choir. We have been invited to perform in Halifax and are undergoing a fundraising campaign to raise ten thousand dollars. The students are motivated to reach their goal.

NOVEMBER 23

The family of schools leadership meeting is an excellent opportunity to share information and learn about the exciting initiatives in the system that assist students to be more successful. Today we are treated to a presentation about the Developmental Reading Assessment (DRA), an assessment resource developed to help teachers to determine whether or not their students are meeting standards, interpret reading progress, plan for further instruction and assess, using a common resource across the board.

Reading is a priority area of concern for our school. We are constantly looking for materials to assist in the assessment and development of this crucial skill. Just last week our literacy convenor attended a workshop on the accelerated reader program. We are exploring this resource as well because it provides the student with the opportunity to test their comprehension level through a computer program.

NOVEMBER 24

A leadership meeting of administrators and convenors provides us with an opportunity to discuss the direction of the school. There is quite a bit of concern that students in general are not attaining the level of achievement we expect of them. There is particular concern around our students' literacy levels, especially their reading. We are all concerned that many of our students don't like to read and don't have a love of learning. As a result every day we struggle to have them learn. How can we change this? What else can we do? We discuss whether there may be too many other activities going on in the school. Perhaps we should restrict the number of clubs and extra curricular opportunities. I am not in favour of this only because I am not sure that this change will produce the desired results. Further, as middle school educators we must meet the social needs of our students and extra-curricular opportunities address those needs. I am a firm believer in the development of emotional intelligence and these types of school-wide opportunities provide students with the tools they need to develop the five components that Daniel Goleman refers to.

We decide to meet again next week to discuss possible actions. I am all for dialogue that is student centred and results oriented. One strategy we discuss is the restructuring of our school day so that there would be a reading period at the beginning of the day. This will require some timetabling adjustments, but the end result would certainly be worth it.

The director of Ontario Implementation: The Learning Equation visited our school today to observe the implementation of the program. We are going to be a host school for the program. This will allow us to showcase the school and train other teachers across the system. We are so committed to this program and what it does for student learning that we are glad to share our expertise.

Evan, our head of science, technology and math, and grade seven teacher Zo, have done a terrific job of getting this up and running in the school. They spent long hours in the summer working out the kinks, researching and ensuring the success of the program in our school. The program required a substantial financial commitment from our superintendent, who also was very impressed with the possibilities it has for student learning.

It should be noted that as impressive as the Learning Equation is, the heart of the program is the teacher/student interaction that takes place in relation to the computer activities. Teachers always accompany their students to the lab, taking note of their students' daily progress and calling students' attention to ways in which their performance is improving.

The Learning Equation is an effective program, but the classroom teacher is the most important element in computer assisted instruction. Properly trained teachers who have a thorough understanding of the program can provide their students with an added dimension in learning. In the end, it is the classroom teacher's creativity, enthusiasm and professional competence that transform instruction into exemplary student achievement.

The director enjoyed her visit and was impressed with the staff member who was doing the lesson. She commented on the outstanding staff that we have at Lawrence Heights. I already know that, but it is always nice to hear it from others that aren't here day to day.

I really don't know what's happening to me lately. Just the other night my friend invited me over to watch some football and hang out a little, but instead of watching the football game, I spent the whole evening discussing daycare for their child. Like myself they recently became parents. Did they ever tick me off: they spend four months researching and test driving cars, but they spend a half hour deciding on a daycare for their child. They told me they are taking their child to the daycare down the street. They don't even know if the centre is licensed or not, which we all know can affect the standard of service given to a child. I asked them a few standard questions, like, "What does the centre do to minimize health risks?" "What is the sanitation policy?" "Do they have a nutritionist?" They both looked at me like I was crazy.

NOVEMBER 29

On Friday (November 24) I had a book launch to celebrate my book, *The Skin I'm In*. There was a great turnout and it was a terrific evening for my family, friends and colleagues. I was particularly touched by a student from our school who attended and says she hasn't been able to put the book down. I have been asked to do some more talks on the book around the city, which is positive. I have also received a number of congratulatory phone calls about the book and people have been asking where they can purchase it.

We have to send a student home today for having a knife and allegedly threatening other students with it. You want to give everyone the benefit of the doubt, but he made reference to the Matti Baranoski situation and feeling unsafe when explaining why he brought the knife to school. The same student decided to chase another student with the knife!

Chapter 4

The More You Read the More You Know

Term 2: December–March

DECEMBER 1

I can't believe it is December already. This morning I meet with the coordinator of continuing education to confirm that our Saturday program will start on January 22. We are going to target our level 1 and 2 learners for an extra opportunity for computer instruction, as well as math and literacy development. We will use the computer-based programs Learning Equation and Accelerated Reader.

It appears that the discussions we are having with our students about throwing rocks at a neighbourhood dog and kicking the fence of the dog's yard have fallen on deaf ears. Today we had an awful incident outside where the dog got loose, after being provoked by one of our students, and chased after Russ who ran and got hit by a car. Luckily, he wasn't seriously injured, but did go to hospital to have some X rays done. Tomorrow we will address the issue through a school-wide assembly—the good, the bad and the very ugly.

DECEMBER 2

Today is a busy day for us at Lawrence. We have our School Council meeting and a special guest from the board of education talks about the outdoor education program. A few parents are reluctant to send their children to the program as they think that it is time off of school. The presenter, Grant, a former colleague of mine who runs an outstanding program, reassures the parents that the focus is educational and it is an opportunity that they shouldn't miss.

Another concern comes from our Muslim parents as their children will be fasting around that time and also need to pray. Grant assures them that accommodations will be made to ensure their religious beliefs are in no way compromised.

I said that I wouldn't do it again, but here I am on Thursday night preparing to sleep at the school. You see the choir will be performing on

CityTV tomorrow morning and we have to be there for 5:30 a.m., which means we have to leave at 4:45 a.m. It becomes a safety issue for a lot of our students who have to walk over to the school at that time in the morning, so we decide to sleep over, rehearse and hang out. It is actually a lot of fun. The students are great and we get all kinds of support from the community and staff at the school cooking and preparing us for the sleepover.

DECEMBER 3

What a performance! The sleepover was all worth it. Our choir delivered an outstanding performance on CityTV. It may have been our best performance yet. Back at the school the phone is ringing off the hook with people congratulating us and inquiring about our upcoming concert.

I really have to thank Dr. Carmaine Marine, Franklin Robb, Tim Skinner, Keith Goddard and Noel Farrell for all of their hard work. Keeping the choir together has been very challenging because of the progress reports. Students know they need all "yes" on their progress reports to be in the choir. As a result the composition is constantly changing, but somehow, some way, Dr. Marine and company manage to bring it all together and make us all proud. Well Done!

It looks like we have the final pieces together for our Saturday program to start in January.

Literacy Life and Tech 2000

Literacy for Life will target students who are reluctant readers; it promotes a love of reading and learning. It will foster a sense of confidence in the participants and teach them that no matter what they want to do in life, everything requires an ability to read. Participants will be provided with learning opportunities with the Adolescent Literacy Project program, First Steps, the Accelerated Reader Program, book talks and guest readers.

Throughout the program participants will be exposed to a variety of literary genre, such as fiction, drama, biography and poetry and they will learn the comprehension skills needed to appreciate and understand each.

Tech 2000 will promote a love of learning through technology. Participants will be provided with the opportunity to acquire skills in organization of information, manipulating and analyzing data, researching via CD-Rom software and on-line searching; composing and editing written products and developing electronic presentations. They will also be using the Learning Equation which is a highly interactive math program that moves step by step through concepts, allowing the students to learn at their own pace.

We are privileged at Lawrence Heights to be among a group of educators who are willing to provide the level of commitment, dedication and energy needed to initiate and maintain a Saturday program to keep the students of Lawrence Heights on the road to success.

DECEMBER 7

I was asked to speak today at our home high school's staff meeting. I talked a lot about the vision and the mission of the school. Their staff is particularly interested in our uniform policy, which is having a really positive impact on our school climate. They are trying to make some changes and have asked us to work with them to settle some of their students who are our former students. Our guidance counsellor has been spending time over there lending a hand. He has a great rapport with many of the students they are concerned about.

An article in the newspaper about the shooting of a twenty-three year old in the course of a robbery at the Just Desserts restaurant has angered many students, staff and community members. The negative depiction of our community is something that we are all concerned about. The three men standing trial are from the community and attended our school and later Bathurst Heights. We all take exception to the so-called "ugly boxes" people in Lawrence Heights live in and the reference to the rough and tumble neighbourhood where being able to "fight is not a bad thing." Students and staff have decided to respond by inviting the writer to the school and through a letter writing campaign.

DECEMBER 8

Student morale is at an all time high today. Perhaps the video dance party has something to do with it. We end the day with a dance for charity after winning a national contest. Because half the proceeds of the dance will be going to a charity of our school's choosing, we decided to allow all students to attend. This is a big time break for students who don't have all "yes" on their progress report and they know it. The great thing is we raise more than $600, half of which will go to Covenant House, a place for teens to go when they are having difficulty in their life.

DECEMBER 10

Today is the official day of reporting to students' parents. For this report it is an expectation that each teacher meets with every parent of students in her or his class. Because of the ongoing communication we have emphasized and reinforced through our progress reports, there should be no surprises for the parents.

I am touched by a conference that I am asked to sit in on with our Literacy Enrichment Academic Program (L.E.A.P.) teacher and a student who has only been in the country for three years but has done exceptionally well at learning the language. The student always carries a dictionary around with him and has an unbelievable thirst for knowledge. We are very proud of what he has accomplished in the short time he has been here. We congratulate him and his very supportive mother and younger sister. WOW!

After a day of parent interviews—and we had a good turnout—it is time to party. The holiday get-together is a terrific success. It is nice to see staff and their families having a relaxing time and socializing. They deserve it. They have worked hard.

DECEMBER 12

The Lawrence Square Mall, which is just around the corner from us, is hosting an International Human Rights Day and we have a strong presence. Our choir delivers another outstanding performance and our visual arts teacher has a terrific display of student work. We are very proud of our students and the progress they are making. I am stopped and congratulated by a number of parents, but also by people from the community who are amazed by what they are hearing about Lawrence Heights. I am inspired by their responses.

DECEMBER 13

We are devastated to learn that one of our students from last year has been charged with sexual assault. He was a delight to be around while at Lawrence Heights. A well-rounded, intelligent young man—what went wrong? We need to get more information and the circumstances of his arrest because this one is too difficult to swallow. Our guidance counsellor, who bent over backwards for this individual, is obviously taking this hard. I try to console him and tell him it's not his fault. It just seems that more students are coming into contact with the criminal justice system these days for making bad decisions.

DECEMBER 14

An evening performance by the choir is once again outstanding. This performance is for the African Heritage Educators Network, a group that provides support and the opportunity to network among educators of African heritage.

DECEMBER 15

We suspend a student today for bringing a replica gun to school. We have talked about this as a school with our students and we treat it very seriously.

The focus of today's staff meeting is school policies. We need to determine how we will proceed in the new year. I also bring up the issue of restructuring our school day to include a reading period at the start of every day. Staff are split on the issue, which I find surprising. Convenors have expressed concern with the overall literacy rates of our students and want to develop a plan of action that will touch all of our students. The questions raised by staff are relevant and solvable. I just expected to hear more enthusiasm for the philosophy of the proposal. I have always believed that if something is educationally sound then it is administratively possible.

Not to make excuses, but the time of the year probably has a lot to do with it. The staff have worked hard and are tired. We left the issue with the convenors to revisit in their team meetings. I have always prided myself on being a leader who doesn't sit around and complain but believes in doing something.

DECEMBER 16

I am greeted this morning by the parent of Donnohue, a former student. She presents me with a beautiful plaque that reads, "certificate of appreciation presented to Dr. Spence, Tim Skinner and staff for outstanding and dedicated service at Lawrence Heights from Donnohue and family." Needless to say we are all touched by the gesture. It is comforting to know we have made a difference in Donnohue's life. He is now doing very well, bravo!

A student of ours has to be sent home for the remainder of the year. Tom and Terri have been interviewing female students in the school around allegations of what amounts to sexual harassment. Allegedly this student has been touching some of the girls inappropriately and making some suggestive and sexual comments. Tom is working on a plan to get some counselling for the youngster; he has a history of this kind of conduct.

It has been a busy week for the choir. A performance at the Jamaican Canadian Centre was a huge success. As part of our performance we served their seniors lunch. It was a terrific experience to have our young people interact with the seniors group.

DECEMBER 17

Steve and Sandy's act at our school crashed to an end today. The brother made some disgusting comments to another student, "the only reason you got to go is because you sucked his (the teacher's) dick," then refused to accept responsibility or to leave the school. The situation became ugly when he made death threats to a staff member and student. The police were called and he was charged and picked up. He has to spend the night in custody.

It is quite sad to see this end this way, but I really do believe that we have done all that we can to help him. He has been to my house several times, has access to my phone number and was shown a lot of love. Tom has gone beyond the call of duty to show this kid some love, so we are all hurting right now wondering what the hell went wrong.

Sandy is also at the end of the line. She came in a couple of days ago and refused to do anything and made some rude comments to staff. This is after she just returned from a ten-day suspension! Clearly, she too needs a new environment. She has exhausted everything we as a school have to offer.

DECEMBER 19

I spoke to Steve and Sandy's mother today. We are very concerned about them, and she is really at the end of the line as well. She informs me that Steve's father put up the bail for him and the youngster isn't taking the incident very seriously. He is due back in court this week so we can only sit tight and wait right now.

DECEMBER 23

On the way into work this morning the radio is playing "She Gives Me Joy," one of the favourite songs of my wife, Marcia, and I. It certainly has me reflecting on just how lucky I am to have such a supportive partner. We enjoy each other. We trust each other. We rely on each other.

So I just want to say in a very public way that I deeply adore, respect and admire Marcia. She has supported me through more pipe dreams than I even have time to list. She has been there for me in every sense of the world. She loves Lawrence Heights as much as I do and has routinely welcomed the staff and students into our home.

I wish you could know her the way students and staff do and could see the light in her eyes when she worked tirelessly to help put on our fashion show. However, you'll have to settle for these meagre second-hand words and impressions from someone who knows.

Now, don't get me wrong. Things haven't always been easy. The late night phone calls, the long days and the bringing of work home certainly took its toll at times, but she is raising and nurturing our children, keeping our home and keeping the faith, and I thank her for that.

The break is finally here. The staff and students have worked hard and deserve a restful holiday. The last couple of days have been filled with anticipation. We had a dance and allowed all who wanted to attend to go—this made student morale soar. They were so appreciative. It really has me thinking hard about meeting the social needs of middle school students. They need more of these kinds of opportunities for socialization and interaction.

I am flattered by the gifts, cards and well wishes for the holiday season for my family and me. Special attention is given to our five-month-old daughter, Briana, who has now received five beautiful stuffed animals.

•••

JANUARY 10

We're back. Clearly the holiday has everyone feeling re-energized and ready to go. My morning starts with a parent meeting to address the concerns of a student who had to be sent home before the break for making sexual comments to female students at the school. The student's stepfather is a reasonable man and understands our concerns. Part of the problem, according to his stepfather, is that they have been reducing his medication for Attention Deficit Disorder, but now feel that he will have to remain on it. He shares some strategies with us that are effective at home and we all agree to work together for his son's success.

I am saddened to hear that one of our students, Steve, had a rough time over the holidays. He is the same student who uttered death threats late last year. Apparently this time he went on a stealing binge and has been detained.

School Report: How Are We Doing?

Safe School Environment—Grade B
A safe school is a shared responsibility. We are still concerned with before and after school unsupervised time, walking in the middle of the street going home and issues of respect.

Opportunities—Grade A+
Lawrence Heights continues to offer numerous opportunities for students to excel. Students can join student council or attend outings to Tech 2000, Literacy for Life, Gifted Readers Club, YTV, Detroit, Windsor, Brian McKnight and Destiny's Child concert, and the list goes on and on.

Talent—Grade B+
Unused talents give you no advantage whatsoever over someone who has no talent at all. We have an extremely talented student body at our school; however, there needs to be more preparation and discipline. Students need to realize that without a positive attitude and effort, talent means nothing. Some of our most talented individuals are not able to represent the school because they have not met the academic and social expectations of the school.

School Tone—Grade A-
The school tone refers to the positive/negative vibes one gets when entering and visiting the school. We have come a long way in this regard, but everyone, including our superintendent, trustee, parents, executive council member and the Toronto Star newspaper, all agree

that when you enter our school you realize that something special is happening.

We do have areas of concern, particularly before and after school when students aren't being supervised.

Academic Achievement—Grade C

"Wise people learn whenever they can. Fools learn when they must." I ask all students to reflect on this quote because the academic achievement of our students is not what it needs to be. The evidence is the lack of level 3 and 4 learners (B and A students), which should be approximately 25 percent of our students.

Commitment to Learning

Do the students of Lawrence Heights have a love of learning? Do they have a thirst for knowledge? The answer is no. We have at this point more talkers than doers. I remind our students it's not just the will to succeed it's the will to prepare to succeed that separates the talkers from the doers.

Our motto for 2000:
The more you read
The more you know
The more you know
The further you go!

Students at Lawrence Heights must commit themselves to reading more because reading is to the mind what exercise is to the body.

We will also make use of our level 3 and 4 students as role models for the upcoming year and get them to articulate to their peers what makes a great student.

At today's school assembly we revisit the goals that we set in September. We have diligently charted our progress and today serves as a reminder as to where we are as a school. We start the assembly with the following motto: Motivation is what gets you started. HABIT is what keeps you going.

JANUARY 11

It's only the second day back and we have to send a student home for violating our safe school policy. Two students reported that Zack, our student, had purchased a lighter over the lunch hour and stole another one and had them at school. The student did admit to having one of the lighters. The situation escalated when we made a phone call home as Zack has had some issues with starting fires and is not to have matches or lighters in his possession.

We were later advised by his teacher that he has been up on arson charges as he and a friend set fire to a neighbour's fence.

Staff and students are all busy getting ready for our celebration of Martin Luther King's birthday on Monday. We are hosting the Martin's day celebration and are looking forward to a terrific day.

JANUARY 14

An appearance on *Off The Record* yesterday on the Total Sports Network (TSN) was a great opportunity for me to talk a little bit about my first book and talk sports. A staff member called to let me know that the message I gave came through loud and clear to someone he has been working with who has vowed to return to school. That was great to hear.

JANUARY 17

Today we open our doors to the whole city to celebrate Martin's day. It is an incredible day. We have a thousand students and staff participate in a morning and afternoon program. Local TV cover the event. Musical performances, storytelling, student displays and the open-mic session allow students and staff to articulate what Martin Luther King means to them. All in attendance are truly touched and impressed with the quality of speakers during the session. I am so proud to be the principal of Lawrence Heights. Bravo!

JANUARY 18

Our grade 8 students went to see the movie the *Hurricane* today. The Hurricane of course is Rubin Hurricane Carter, the former number one contender for the World Middleweight Title until he was falsely accused and convicted of murder. This all took place back in 1966 in Patterson, New Jersey, when two lying criminals said that they witnessed Hurricane Carter and an accomplice kill the bartender at the Lafayette Bar and Grill. Apparently the bartender was known to sometimes refuse service to Black patrons. Rubin spent twenty years behind bars for a crime he didn't commit. In the end justice prevailed, but what the hell happened?

The grade 8 students all had an emotional reaction to the film, which is good. The majority of them came back to the school significantly different. Even if it is for a short time, the film did have an impact. It won't stop there for them as they will be reading the novel, discussing it further and doing follow-up assignments as part of their Language Arts.

It is worth mentioning that I have recently contracted an eye infection. Both of my eyes are bloodshot and quite honestly I look a mess. The degree to which the students in this school are concerned with my well-being just amazes me. I even had one student start crying, asking me if I was going die. They stop constantly in the hall advising me what to do and telling me it's okay to go home because they will be fine.

JANUARY 19

An emotional meeting today with Steve and Sandy's mother. Their mother is now insisting that her daughter stay at our school. It looked like a done deal, that she would start the school year somewhere else, but things have deteriorated at home and Sandy's mother thinks that by allowing her to go to another school things will only get worse.

I feel that we have exhausted everything at this school for both of her children. Steve will be moving on to another school, but we all agree to give her daughter another opportunity. The whole situation has left me second guessing myself, but when I see this young lady and all the anger she has, it breaks my heart. This is the reason most of us got into education—we believe that we could turn around the difficult ones that most people give up on.

Our staff meeting today focuses on emotional intelligence. Our guest speaker is Carol Tumber, who has forged an identity for herself as an expert on the topic. The presentation is well received by staff who are eager to learn more about how we can help our students be more successful.

JANUARY 20

Today we hosted the playoffs for boys basketball. Our team won both of their games and will advance to the championship game next Friday. We try to make these occasions into opportunities to build school spirit by filling the gym with our students during our games. The students love to come and cheer on their peers.

JANUARY 21

Toronto Raptors' Alvin Williams and Kevin Willis visited our school today as part of their slam-dunk school violence campaign. After their presentation we gave away some of the Raptor shirts and hats to outstanding citizens in and around the school. I am particularly warmed by the actions of a young man who helped a caretaker on the last day of school until after 5 o'clock. The caretaker was so appreciative of his help because she was on duty all by herself, that she offered to give him some money. He refused saying he did it from the heart and didn't want any money. Now that is nice.

JANUARY 22

It is Saturday, but we are here today to kick off our Saturday programs Literacy for Life and Tech 2000. It is a bitterly cold day but we have a great turnout that includes the coordinating principal, our trustee, our superintendent, staff, students and parents. We were all warmed up by the dynamic and insightful storytelling of community member Sandra Whiting, who delivered a great performance.

I often wonder if we at Lawrence Heights are squandering the gifts, talents and interests of many of our students. The students I am referring to are our high achieving students who have a broad range of intellectual and artistic talents and may not be challenged to do their best work. The problem can be especially severe in disadvantaged communities, where we often find the majority of our students playing catch up. As a result these high achieving students have access to fewer advanced educational opportunities and their talents may go unnoticed.

Reforming our schools depends on challenging students to work harder and master more complex material. Few would argue against this for students performing at low or below grade levels. But we must also challenge our top performing students to greater heights.

Today, researchers know that intelligence takes many forms and therefore many criteria need to be used to measure it. This understanding has led educators to question traditional definitions of intelligence and current assessment practices and procedures. We must identify outstanding talent and nurture that talent by observing students in settings that enable them to display their abilities, rather than relying solely on test scores. It is my opinion that all of our students, including the most able, can learn more than we now expect. But it will take a major commitment for this to occur.

JANUARY 24

We have an assembly today to kick off our Read-A-Thon. This marks another opportunity to stimulate our students to read. The Read-A-Thon is being sponsored by the Multiple Sclerosis Society, which is a worthy cause. A representative from the society gave an informative presentation that gives all of us a better understanding of this serious disability.

I decide to make this a mandatory school event so that all students participate by reading and getting sponsors.

JANUARY 26

Our math consultant visits the school today to begin preparations for us to host the Math Olympics in April. This is a great opportunity for our school to demonstrate that our focus is academics. There still tends to be a perception that we are more athletic than academic.

I am co-chairing a committee for our family of schools to address our EQAO scores. Today's meeting produces many excellent suggestions we can undertake, such as examining best practices, identifying master teachers, and sharing and obtaining resources. All agree that we only need to work smarter and not necessarily harder.

JANUARY 27

I am disappointed to hear that a number of our students did not make good decisions last night at the Raptors game. This is the third game that we have taken a hundred students to and previously there hadn't been an incident. Today I sent four students home and consequenced a whole lot more. The four grade 8 students set a poor example for our grade 6 students. The fact that one of them is our student council president is really disappointing—he tried to buy beer and sign up for a VISA card. It is also disappointing that three students on the boys' basketball team will not be able to play in the championship game tomorrow. Further, we had to send a teacher to pick up two female students who were playing in a girls' tournament across the city. If they can't conduct themselves in an appropriate manner they cannot represent our school.

JANUARY 28

Lawrence Heights really is an exciting place to be and a great place to learn. Today we are hosting the Blueprints for Life seminar concert that features break dancers, rapping, hip hop music, a free style competition, free giveaways, autograph signing and discussions on graffiti art, explicit music lyrics, youth violence, education and the state of hip hop music. We have a positive afternoon with some extraordinarily talented young people.

During the presentation the boys' basketball team arrived with a silver medal. They lost in overtime. Many return to the school crying and hanging their heads in disappointment. We do our best to cheer them up and eventually get the emcee for the Blueprints for Life to invite the team up to the stage and congratulate them for a terrific season. The student body shows their appreciation and gives them a rousing applause.

An informal after school chat session with some staff has me thinking. I started the discussion because of what I perceive to be a lack of appreciation for all we do around here. You would be hard pressed to find another school that meets the social and academic needs of students the way we do. Maybe it was just a bad week, maybe we are feeling a little discouraged because of what happened at the Raptors game. Anyway, Monday is a new day.

JANUARY 29

It is hard to believe that today is Saturday. The school is very busy. We have Saturday school, fashion show auditions and music rehearsal. I wonder if these students realize how lucky they are?

I am saddened to hear Thomas Beans Bowles, who played the saxophone and flute on several Motown hits, passed away last night of prostate cancer at seventy-three. He contributed to several classic Motown hits including, Marvin Gaye's "Stubborn Kind of Fellow" and "What's Going On" and the Vandellas' "Heat Wave" and the Supremes' hit "Baby Love." Beans visited our school at the request of our guidance counsellor and was present when our choir performed at the Motown Museum. He often spoke to students from our school on the phone and developed a passion for our students. Thank you Beans, you will be missed.

JANUARY 30

Our choir puts on another outstanding performance today, this time for the Ontario Black History Society's brunch. It is a terrific event that features George Elliott Clark, a seventh generation Canadian who has published three books and has been honoured as a poet and an activist scholar. Also in attendance are His Honour Lincoln M. Alexander, who was formerly lieutenant governor of Ontario; Judge Stanley Grizzle, formerly a citizenship judge and author of *My Name's George;* and Anthony Sherwood, an actor, writer and film producer who created a film project, *Paths of Glory—Across the Country in Ten Heroes.*

JANUARY 31

This morning our trustee, Sheine Mankosky, drops by to donate *Dreamcast* to our school. *Dreamcast* is the newest game console developed by SEGA Enterprises Limited, which integrates communication functions so that users can access the internet from their television sets. This is going to look great in our games room and it is something the students are going to love.

FEBRUARY 1

Today marks the beginning of Black History Month. It is the month in which we bear witness to the progress, richness and diversity of African Canadian/American achievement. During the 1920s an African American named Carter G. Woodson created and promoted Negro History Week. This period in February was chosen because it included the birthdays of Fredrick Douglass and Abraham Lincoln. In 1976 the month-long celebration was implemented as a time for everyone to reflect on both the history and teachings of African Canadians/Americans. Like many schools, this is something we celebrate year round. Today, however we have a special kick-off with the theatrical performance, "The Spirit of Harriet Tubman," performed by Leslie McCurdy. "The Spirit of Harriet Tubman" tells stories beginning with her being hired out at the age of six. Then it follows her solo flight from slavery, her involvement with the underground railroad, her victorious rescue mission in the civil war and her continued commitment to others in her later years. It is an amazing performance, tarnished only by the response of some of our students who do not want to pay the two dollars to attend. That really hurts.

FEBRUARY 3

It has been a busy week at Lawrence and our student body's decision-making has been less than spectacular. I don't know if it is the time of year or what, but there has been something in the air. For example, today we had to have all students get their coats and go back outside when the bell rang because of the way they had entered the building (pushing and shoving). They were none too pleased, but needed to be reminded that safety comes first.

FEBRUARY 4

Our grade 6 basketball team represented us very well in our tournament. In fact they won the championship. I am very pleased with the comments from parents, coaches and players from visiting schools who are impressed with the way our student athletes conduct themselves, and with the school itself. We have done a terrific job in making Lawrence Heights an inviting place, so it is nice for all of us to be complimented. The student athletes are humble in victory and demonstrate the epitome of sportspersonship. I give full credit to their coaches, who have done an outstanding job coaching and mentoring our students.

Lunar New Year is celebrated this year on Saturday, February fifth, but we'll start our discussions with our students today and have an announcement about it at the start of the day. And, as part of our Saturday program, we have invited a Chinese musician to our school to kick-off our celebrations.

Staff will also take time to discuss with students that this is the year of the dragon. Lunar New Year is a religious and cultural celebration for many Chinese, Vietnamese and Koreans, regardless of country or religion. This is the year 4698 according to the Chinese calendar.

The Lawrence Heights Boys Student Athlete Roundball Classic got under way today. It is the second year in a row that we have hosted this international tournament. The feature team is the Post Middle School Rams from Detroit, Michigan. We have developed a terrific relationship with Post that involves various exchanges. In the fall we visited their school with our choir, and we are participating in a pen pal program with their students. It is great to see the students interacting in such a positive way. Their school is much like ours so it is enlightening to speak to their principal, Benjamin Purkett, who has a wealth of experience and knowledge that he willingly shares. In the short time that I have known him he has greatly touched me with his philosophy and his commitment to his students and staff.

The Post Rams did not disappoint—their team was outstanding. They won and won big, and put on a halftime show that rivals the SuperBowl. With tumblers, steppers and cheerleaders, it was a magnificent day. Not to be outdone were our steppers, who were amazing. Anytime you get a standing ovation from a pretty tough crowd you know you did something right. Once again I have to give full credit to teachers Wayne Dawkins and Charmaine Marine for pulling it all together and making us very proud.

FEBRUARY 5

The Post Rams defended their title and won for the second straight year. The whole entourage (they brought fifty-five students, staff and parents) displayed excellent sportspersonship. It was great to hear that members of their honour society (outstanding academic students) were also on the trip.

A big congratulations has to go out to the staff and students of Lawrence Heights for hosting the best middle school tournament around. A special thanks goes out to the coaches for running such a well organized tournament. Win or lose, all those in attendance and participating had a great time. Monday we will start preparations for our girls' tournament.

Two staff members attended the funeral for Beans Bowles on Saturday. Motown legends Stevie Wonder and Ester Gordy Edwards were among the hundreds of musicians, friends and family members who celebrated the esteemed musician's life. He certainly made an impact on the students and staff who he touched at our school. In fact, a letter that one of our students wrote to him was read at the funeral.

FEBRUARY 7

Today we welcome our replacement for Terri, who is off on maternity leave. We introduce Keon, through our grade team assemblies. Keon brings a wealth of experience and knowledge, which I am sure will serve us all well.

There is still a buzz in the building about the tournament over the weekend. It was a huge success and preparations are underway to do it all over again for our girls' tournament.

I am angered that one of our students had to be sent home today for abusing one of our school pets. Our pet project provides students with the opportunity to care for pets (dogs, guinea pigs, a rabbit and a ferret) and to learn responsibility. This particular student found it funny to throw things at the guinea pig and listen to him squeal!

FEBRUARY 8

Two male students at our school are in need of some love. One of them comes to the office glassy eyed and tells me his parents are going to divorce. The other student I am alerted to is missing his mother who has gone home to Eritrea for six months. A tough situation for a youngster to deal with.

With all that is happening in education today the last thing we need is one of our own staff publicly bad mouthing our students in an attempt to indirectly support some of the initiatives put forth by the government. I will call him Mr. Q because I question why he got into teaching in the first place.

Dear Mr. Q:

Children learn about the world not only through acting upon it directly, but through the eyes and ears of parents, teachers and friends. It is through this socialization process that children become members of society, enabling them to share what they see and feel with others. We are all socializing agents for one another. A teacher is more than this for his or her students, however. In addition to the unintended socializing effect that teacher responses may have upon children, teachers influence them as educators as well.

The most disturbing thing about your article is that you claim to be an educator. Your comment, "while [students] seem to be more genial and good natured than ever, they are so ignorant—and so ignorant of their ignorance—that they literally terrify me," makes me wonder how many young minds you have destroyed with this fatalistic attitude. It is adults such as you who can truly interfere with the direction of the education system. Clearly you would prefer to shortcut the socialization process by giving children a set of rules that constitutes good and bad—and setting up a system of rewards based on their acceptance of these rules. It seems it may be difficult for you to realize that process rather than the end product is what needs to be highlighted in our schools. I am sure if your students were able to blurt out formulas, that you would not be quite so free with your statement that "the ability to perform even the simplest computations is just a memory among most students I see." I doubt very much that students in your class are taught that knowledge and process are the source of success; it is individuals like you who undermine our children to the extent that they are conditioned to be dependent upon the approval of others.

Further, it frustrates me to hear you condemn our youth and their shortcomings, rather than build on their strengths. You have chosen to criticize rather than utilize. If you were a tax-paying citizen offering an opinion from the outside, I could respect that, but to be an educator and to have given up on the future and label children "slothful and ignorant" is most disturbing.

Finally, Mr Q, may I refer you to a poem entitled "The Man In The Mirror." Judging from your article, this would be a most enlightening approach for you. The poem suggests that before pointing the finger, before criticizing—take a good look in the mirror—what could have been done differently? Perhaps the most revealing point you make throughout the article is your reference to "students I see." This suggests your view of youth is quite limited.

Once you have reflected on these types of observations, I am confident you will find not a learning disability among today's youth, but a teaching disability in yourself.

Because children learn in different ways, teachers must change their approaches in order to meet the students' immediate needs. Only teacher experimentation, assessment and observation will provide the basis for decisions about what children need. Apparently, the students you see need to be observed as whole students so that you can meet their needs.

I feel much better.

FEBRUARY 14

Love is in the air. We celebrate Valentine's Day with style. For the last couple of weeks students have had the opportunity to purchase cards to be sent to others in the school and today they will be delivered.

I am flattered by the many students who stop by the office with a Valentine's card for me and the rest of the office staff. I am particularly touched by a homemade card from an outstanding student—this reminds me that we are making a difference in their lives. I needed to be reminded of this because students have been restless lately and are not meeting the expectations of the school. The most reasonable of expectations are being dismissed with a very carefree attitude of "who cares." For the most part the problem is with our grade 8 students, who may have their minds on high school rather than middle school, which is something that happens at this time of year.

FEBRUARY 16

It was sad to see two of our grade 7 female students being arrested today. They were both charged with assault for their part in an ugly fight. Although I didn't think it was a police issue, one of the parents felt that she wanted the police involved. When all was said and done both twelve-year-old students, Freda and Kate, were arrested. The police officers on the scene made it very clear that their position is zero tolerance. A recent shooting at a Toronto high school has galvanized this approach.

This incident sent shock waves through the school, so we quickly met with all students through grade assemblies to debrief and revisit our code of behaviour and our safe school plan. We continue to communicate the message that a safe school is a shared responsibility (see Appendix D).

Unfortunately, after the grade 6 assembly two students got into a verbal exchange and were ready to go at it—our message went in one ear and out the other in a matter of seconds.

Freda's parents came by the school and were quite emotional. Freda's mother hadn't been home yet and didn't have all the details. She was obviously devastated and didn't have any answers. To complicate the issue, our guidance counsellor returned with the news that the court order prohibits Freda from returning to this school.

My five o'clock meeting was with a very supportive parent in the community who I called because of some concerns I have about his son, Tyson. Tyson just seems to be off track and doesn't seem to care. A couple of weeks ago he brought some porn magazines to the school and Tom spent a lot of time with him trying to get some answers. Tom cut him a lot of slack and took it as an opportunity to counsel and support with the only stipulation being he had to tell his father what had happened. The youngster agreed and was extremely appreciative of the opportunity. As it turns out he didn't tell his father. I called his father in because I had asked all the grade 8 students, who are having a difficult time settling, to jot down on a piece of paper how they would like the school year and their time at Lawrence to end. Ninety-nine percent of the students responded by saying they want their time at Lawrence to end on a positive note. They want to leave with a sense of accomplishment, pride and dignity knowing that they have worked hard. However, two students took a negative spin on things and said they just don't care. That really hurt because one thing we can't do is make students care. Tyson's father agreed. We ended the meeting by agreeing on yet another opportunity for his son to turn it around. I have always said you sink or swim based on your actions and behaviour.

FEBRUARY 18

At about 9:00 p.m. last night I received a call at home from a student who was hysterical. She said her mother had been stabbed and she didn't know what to do. I calmed her and got her to tell me exactly what was happening. She had already called the police and they had arrived and were at the scene. She was across the road at a neighbour's house and was terrified and just needed someone to talk to. Now that the police were there I encouraged her to go back over to the house because she would have to give them a statement. She did so and was supposed to get back to me to let me know how things were, but didn't. Tom was very concerned and made a trip out to her neighbourhood at midnight but didn't come away with any answers as he didn't have the exact address. The incident made for a difficult night of sleeping.

I was anxious to see if the student would be here in the morning so that I could get the rest of the details. She was at school but only said, "everything is okay now." I decided not to push it any further only asking if anyone was injured, to which she responded, "everyone is okay."

We decided to postpone the belated Valentine's dance given the tone of the school over the last three to four weeks. Hopefully the student body will get back on track really soon.

A visitor from Wilson Public School in Kitchener enjoys her morning at Lawrence Heights. The visit was prompted by the newspaper article in the *Toronto Star* about Lawrence Heights and the subsequent visit by our choir to their school.

FEBRUARY 21

The funeral services for Farah Khan certainly make me think about how we track our students' absences. The five-year-old was found dead in early December, days after her stepmother withdrew her from classes. Once the kindergarten student was withdrawn from her school, nobody knew for sure where she had gone.

What happens is when a student moves from one school to another within a school district a student's records are still in the board's computer system. Therefore, if a student hasn't been formally withdrawn from the system and doesn't show up for classes, school officials will notify the proper authorities that the child is truant. The problem arises however if a student is officially withdrawn from the school board and is no longer the board's responsibility.

Parents are required to notify the school board when they are withdrawing a student from the board, but no one can demand proof of whether a child is really moving out of the district. Farah's stepmother told staff they were withdrawing the child from school because they were moving back to Pakistan. There was no reason to question her explanation and no one was surprised when she didn't return.

I guess we can all learn from this tragedy and perhaps be a little more suspicious especially if a student leaves or is taken out of school.

FEBRUARY 22

Today we hosted our family of schools principal meeting. The first hour of the meeting was devoted to a demonstration and observation of a lesson using the Learning Equation. Zo and her students did an outstanding presentation.

The talk of the meeting, though, was the sad news that Bathurst High School, the home high school for our students, has been recommended for closure. Built in 1951, it has 481 students—only 38 percent of capacity according to ministry guidelines. The plan, to be voted on in the spring, would cut by 650,000 square feet the amount of property for which the board gets no government grants.

FEBRUARY 28

I spent February 24–25 in Halifax participating in an African Heritage Month event sponsored by the Black Community Workgroup of Halifax Cooperative Limited and Human Resources Development of Canada. It gave me an opportunity to discuss my book and to talk about some of the programs we have implemented at Lawrence Heights. The response was quite overwhelming. In fact I met with a number of inner city school principals who would like me to come back and do some workshops with their staff. Given the substantial Black population in Nova Scotia and the underachievement of Black males in the educational system, the issues that I addressed were relevant to their concerns.

On returning to school today I was greeted with the good, the bad and the ugly events that occurred during my absence. The good was the cultural showcase put on by the grade 7 team of staff and students. The show lasted a whopping two hours and featured dance, recitals, a video presentation and a storyteller. Both students and staff were glued to their seats—a good indicator of a successful performance. Congratulations!

At the polar opposite was a situation that escalated to the point that the police had to be called in to intervene. This situation involved one student telling another student that another student had a gun and was going to shoot her. Given what has happened in schools lately with guns and the growing concerns around safety, the police and parents were immediately called. Luckily, the situation was resolved but the seriousness cannot be discounted. Particularly after it was discovered at a local high school that a student had a list of students he wanted to kill. The list has surfaced and that student is now in custody.

FEBRUARY 29

It was a busy day at Lawrence Heights today. Our choir performed at Bathurst High School as part of an African Heritage Month celebration. We sent more than seventy of our students, who thoroughly enjoyed the day and the performances.

We hosted a girl's basketball tournament at our school and our girls were very successful, winning both of their games. It was great to see the student body cheering on our girls.

The Learning Equation was also in operation as staff from other schools were in visiting and observing the program.

I am stunned to hear that in Michigan today a boy shot a six-year-old girl in class. As a parent and an educator it just sends a chill up my spine to think a six-year-old could have access to a gun and do such a thing! It certainly makes us all realize the importance of establishing and reinforcing a code of behaviour and observing our students at all times for unusual behaviour. I really feel for the children, staff and parents involved.

The issue of race does not always get addressed in our schools in ways that are constructive and essential to recreating schools for all children. Race is a very difficult topic for most people to talk about for many reasons. They are afraid of being accused of being racist. They are nervous about saying the wrong thing or using a politically incorrect phrase. Most people find it easier to simply avoid the topic. We, as school leaders, must work harder and more courageously to facilitate blame free environments in which it is safe to discuss this difficult subject. We do not need to point fingers—there is enough blame for all of us. Since race is a key issue to be addressed in our increasingly diverse schools, we must openly and honestly tackle this issue.

MARCH 2

Engaging students in real world problem solving, as they acquire the skills and knowledge needed for success in work and life, is important for middle school learners. One of the many personal transitions middle school students make is that they begin to see that school is preparing them for life. The connections between school and life can be made apparent by providing an interdisciplinary curriculum that is rooted in real world topics that are exciting and timely.

Although most of the curriculum we deliver is mandated, we still try to seek out opportunities for teachers to provide instruction that integrates traditional subjects. Teachers use thematic units as the organizing principle for instruction in agreed upon areas, engage students in projects requiring knowledge and skill across several traditional content areas, make use of other resources, including hands-on materials in addition to textbooks, and use performance assessments that allow students to demonstrate integrated knowledge and skills from several traditional subject areas.

Today was easily one of the most exciting days for me as an educator. A reporter (not the earlier reporter) from the *Toronto Star* visited our school to respond to an article that many of us who work and live in the community feel was not an accurate portrayal of the community (see students' letters). The reporter was given a tour of the school, watched our promotional video and a PowerPoint presentation, and listened to about twenty-five students who voiced their concerns.

It was extremely powerful. I was so proud of our students and the way they handled themselves. The reporter was also impressed with the students and felt the future of the community looked very bright with these articulate young people involved.

MARCH 6

The day starts with an angry parent visiting the school. He is angry with his daughter, Kate, who was involved with that police incident a few weeks back when she and Freda were arrested. She has been ostracized by her peers because of the friendships Freda had with students here and because Freda was ordered through the courts not to return to the school. Well Kate has now taken on the role that it is cool to be bad and has become increasingly defiant and disrespectful, almost as if nothing had ever happened. Her teachers felt it was serious enough that they wanted her father

12/9/99

Dear Philip Mascoll,

My name is Heidy, I'm 13 years old, I go to Lawrence Heights Middle School. I'm writing this letter to you because I disagreed with the way you wrote your article about the "Just Desserts suspects growing up In The City's Concrete Jungle."

First, I don't think you should call the community the "Jungle." That is very inappropriate because people live there, and I really don't think they appreciate you calling their neighbourhood "The Jungle." Secondly, you described how these three families lived within metres of one another in ugly, "concrete boxes." You really didn't have to use the words "ugly" or "concrete boxes" to describe people's homes. Your article also wrote about these particular young men gravitating around the community centre, where they played basketball, lifted weights and practised martial arts. Not all young men in the Lawrence Heights community liked to do all those things in their spare time. There are a lot of other things a young man can do there which you failed to mention.

When you wrote your article, why did you make "The Jungle" seem like such a bad neighbourhood? You made it seem like it was a very dangerous area to live in. Most students in my class live in those "concrete boxes," and they are not bad people. I really don't like the way you described their neighbourhood.

I didn't write this letter to criticize you or tell you about the mistakes you wrote in you article, but next time I believe you should write about the good as well as the bad to give your readers a full portrayal of any community. I would also like to extend an invitation to you to come visit Lawrence Heights Middle School and address all the students here. I would enjoy your visit.

Yours Truly
Heidy

to come and assist us in getting her back on track. Kate's father didn't take the news well at all and made it very clear to her that she would not like what would happen if he heard anything like this again.

Tears were shed and the student appeared to have understood the very strong message she was given by her father, or so we thought. Later

December 9, 1999

Dear Philip Mascoli,

Hello, my name is Mustafa Rahmanzadeh and I am a grade 8 Afghan student at Lawrence Heights Middle School. My concerns with the article that you've written was how you've describe the Flemington / Lawrence Heights community.

My first concern with your article is how you describe the homes of many people who live in the LH community. Why were you so focused on the nagativities of the "Jungle"?

My second concern was how you described that most of the people who live in the LG community are West Indian. You are wrong. There are many other nationalities living here such as Afghans, Vietnamese, Spanish, Chinese, etc. You see there is a wide variety of people living in LH not just West Indians. By visiting my school you must have a greater understanding of the different cultures in our community. Describing the homes in LH as "boxes" is a very negative way to describe where people live and how they raise their children.

The article was a very negative way to tell the people of Toronto that they should not come to the LH community. Not everyone in this community steals, kills, or beats up others. These three individuals made very bad choices for themselves and their families but the whole community should not be painted with the same brush. I think you should know there are many positive things that happen in our community and that most of the people who live here are honest and hard-working people.

Sincerely,
Mustafa

that day she was again involved in another situation of writing and passing around extremely rude and disgusting notes about another student!

MARCH 7

Kate, the same student whose father came in yesterday, was to spend the day in the office, but there was something strange about her mannerism today. She wouldn't take her coat off, which seemed weird, and she kept asking for ice. She wouldn't give a reason when she was asked why she wanted the ice. The office staff alerted us that something wasn't right.

Shortly thereafter she disclosed to our guidance counsellor that she had been awakened at midnight from her bed and beaten by her mother as a result of her father having to visit the school. She had some long red welts on her arm and was still blaming the school for calling her dad.

As it turned out we had to call Children's Aid, who in turn called the police. The mother was charged and the youngster was removed from the home. Days like this are so difficult—they are emotionally draining for all of us and they just tug at your heart. What when wrong? Here was a student that was new to the school, doing well in the classroom, performing in the choir and playing on the basketball team, and now this?

For the first few days Kate resided in a group home and called the school almost every day. She spoke to Tom for support. He too was shaken by the incident, particularly when he accompanied her to the police station and they took a look at her back. "It was like 'Roots' all over again," he said with a tremor in his voice. He later went out and bought her a stuffed teddy bear, which I know she greatly appreciated.

MARCH 9

At today's recognition assembly we celebrate our Academic All Stars—the top ten students at each grade level. We also celebrate and recognize the most improved students and, in what has become a tradition, we celebrate our teachers. Today I invite our superintendent to attend and present our teachers with T-shirts that read:

Believing In Achieving
Lawrence Heights Middle School

The assembly is a great success. Presenters from Positive Impact also join us. Their organization recognizes people from the community at large for the positive contributions that they make. Today they recognize a student who has been very helpful in and around the school, and I am recognized.

The Millennium Fashion Show is a huge success. Staff, students and Marcia, my wife, put in long hours to ensure its success. We had sponsors such as Winners, 4th Quarter and Chand's Custom Tailoring and Embroidery. The uniform scenes are great and show that even when wearing a uniform you can have a sense of style. Half of the proceeds from the event go to Covenant House, the largest youth shelter in Canada.

MARCH 10

The March break has come quickly, but I am glad it's here because it has been a busy, busy term. We end the term by having a dance. Instead of progress reports, teachers decide who can attend, thus the majority of students take part and morale is sky high. A great way to end the term.

The break will give me some time to reflect on the highs and lows of the past term, on what we could do differently, and on something I have been thinking about a lot lately—public education. Is it just rhetoric that assumes our public education system offers every child an equal chance to achieve? Our society's sense of justice and fairness is at the root of this issue. In spite of this, schools generally tend to promote the children of advantage and discourage those of disadvantage. The schools play their part in sorting out the successes and failures, and the successes generally come from "good" families and speak with the proper accents. Yet the rhetoric continues to maintain that the public school is the instrument for achieving an equitable society. To abandon this rhetoric would force us to recognize social, ethnic and racial classes.

At its best, equal educational opportunity promises that the doors to success and prosperity will be opened to all of us; that each of us has equal rights and opportunities to develop our own talents and virtues; and that there should be equal rewards for equal performances. But what happens to the individual whose talents are not recognized? Is this inequality based partly on natural inequalities? Equality of educational opportunity for all to develop their capacities is misleading. The fact remains that not all talents can be developed equally in any given society. Out of the great variety of human resources available to it, a given society will admire some abilities more than others.

"Every society has a set of values, and these are arranged in a hierarchy. Genetic endowment is unequal between individuals. Some are more mentally and physically dexterous than others. The differential advantage that it confers upon them cannot be deserved by those fortunate individuals; they did not do anything for their gifts" (Green 1988: 23).

Scharr's rhetorical question still holds force:

> What is so generous about telling a man he can go as far as his talents will take him when his talents are meagre? Imagine a footrace of one mile in which ten men compete, with rules being the same for all. Three of the competitors are forty years old, five are overweight, one has weak ankles, and the tenth is Roger Bannister. What sense does it make to say that all ten have an equal opportunity to win the race? (Scharr 1967: 123)

There is nothing equal about this opportunity. Education itself is a value judgement. Robert Ennis demonstrates this with the use of the following case study:

> Edward Tudor and Tom Canty, born on the same day, were raised respectively in the Palace of Westminster and Offal Court. Edward had a series of private tutors who gave him a strong academic

education. Tom learned by experience in the streets of London. The Earl of Hertford deemed the education of each fitting. (Ennis 1976: 11)

This goes to show that one's judgement about whether there is equality of educational opportunity depends at least in part upon one's judgement about what constitutes an education. In most equal opportunity contexts, this determination requires a value judgement.

Now don't get me wrong, I still believe that schooling that is free and open equally to all is essential. Beyond this concern of equity is the concern that young people of talent and ingenuity should be developed to the fullest. The challenge is to ensure the elimination of any dependency between opportunity and personal background. But is this possible in schools that are mirrors of society? We all want to believe that all Canadians possess a basic equality of opportunity in our society, but many groups do not participate proportionately in those areas considered most economically rewarding and politically powerful. Statistics confirm these inequities, therefore discourse around equality of educational opportunity needs to continue. To forfeit this rhetoric of equality through the schools would destroy our vision of liberty and justice for all.

MARCH 19

We have spent a lot of time getting our school's submission for the National Quality Institute's Canada Awards together, but it has been a great exercise for all of us. It gave us an opportunity to step back and do a gap analysis with the Quality Principles to see where we are. In the process we have learned much about our school and the need to strive for continuous improvement. To be even considered for an award, the school must show outstanding continuous achievement in seven key areas:

- Process optimization
- Supplier focus
- Organizational performance
- Customer focus
- People focus
- Leadership
- Planning for improvement

The choir and the staff involvement with the choir is another example of the great things at Lawrence Heights. Over the March break staff members drove choir members down to the studio where the choir is cutting a CD. Can you imagine—staff willingly giving their time over the break! I am so impressed.

To recognize their commitment, Marcia and I hosted a luncheon for the choir members before heading down to the studio. It really is going to be a fabulous piece of work when it is all completed. We have to give thanks to Dr. Marine for pulling it all together. My singing career didn't last long as I was literally laughed out of the studio, but it was fun.

MARCH 23

The problems persist with Steve and Sandy. Sandy has been in and out of school and regularly comes to school refusing to do anything. We have counselled, supported and encouraged Sandy and there has been little or no progress. Although Steve no longer goes to school here, he has been arrested again for uttering death threats against me and a couple of others on staff (which he does through his friends who do go to this school). He was arrested and charged with the same thing a few months back.

Believe it or not I still think that all individuals have the power to change. Lifton identifies resilience as the human capacity of all individuals to transform and change, no matter what their risks (Lifton 1994); it is an innate "self righting mechanism" (Werner and Smith 1992: 202). Resilience skills include the ability to form relationships (social competence), to problem solve (metacognition), to develop a sense of identity (autonomy), and to plan and hope (a sense of purpose and future). To no one's surprise both of these students are lacking resilience skills, and that may partially explain the difficulties they are having. It also suggests a course of future action for us as a school to further research.

A common finding in resilience research is that teachers have the power to tip the scale from risk to resilience. Teachers provide and model three protective factors that buffer risk and enable positive development by meeting youth's basic needs for safety, love and belonging, respect, power, accomplishment and learning, and ultimately, for meaning (Benard 1991). The factors are these:

Caring Relationships
Teachers can convey loving support to students by listening to students and validating their feelings, and by demonstrating kindness, compassion and respect (Higgins 1994; Meier 1995). They refrain from judging and do not take a student's behaviour personally, understanding that youth are doing the best they can, based on the way they perceive the world.

Positive and High Expectations
Teachers' high expectations can structure and guide behaviour, and can also challenge students beyond what they believe they can do (Delpit 1996). Effective teachers recognize students' strengths, mirror them, and help students see where they are strong. They especially assist overwhelmed students, who have often been labelled or oppressed by their families, other students and sometimes staff, and/or commu-

nity. Teachers can help these students to not take personally the adversity in their lives; not see adversity as permanent; and not see setbacks as pervasive (Seligman 1995). These teachers are student centred; they use students' own strengths, interests, goals and dreams as the beginning point for learning. They tap students' intrinsic motivation for learning.

Opportunities to Participate and Contribute
Effective teachers let students express their opinions and imagination, make choices, problem solve, work with and help others, and give their gifts back to the community. They treat students as responsible individuals by allowing them to participate in all aspects of the school's functioning. (Rutter et al. 1979; Rutter 1984: 57–65; Kohn 1993)

This whole situation with Sandy and Steve has certainly made me reflect on our role as a school in developing caring relationships, not only between educators and students but also between students, between educators, and between educators and parents. We need to know our students to better understand their behaviour so that we can meet their individual needs.

MARCH 24

The staff put their unbeaten record on the line today for the staff–student basketball game. Let's just say we are still undefeated and a great time was had by all.

Chapter 5

Believing in Achieving

Term 3: April–June

APRIL 3

Academic April is officially underway. Our grade 6 team of staff and students are in full preparation mode for the provincial exams in May. Our grade 7 and 8 students will also be assessed. As a school we are trying to take the lead with an initiative to meet the needs of our grade 8 students. The means of assessment is called Project 8 and it is an assessment that resembles the grade 3 and 6 Education Quality Accountability Office assessment (EQAO), but focuses on literacy and math for grade 8 students.

Katherine Anderson Schaffner from the Marvellettes visited our school today. As you know, we have been doing a lot stuff around Motown and had the opportunity to visit and perform at Hitsville in Detroit. Our guidance counsellor was able to strike up a friendship with her and thus her visit. We have become concerned with the attendance of choir members and she gave them a good old fashioned talking to that hit home. She also found time to do some girl talk with a youngster who recently lost her grandmother.

APRIL 4

Congratulations to the girls' basketball team members and their coaches. They qualified for the league final with impressive victories in the playoffs.

A parent dropped by a huge tub of chicken and rice for Marcia and I. She is one of the best cooks in the neighbourhood and regularly sends some of her finger licking good food to enjoy.

As part of Academic April our SOAR program gets set to take off. SOAR is designed to redress the gap in academic success rates between high achieving and under achieving students. The program uses mathematics as the key to achieving educational equity. It is comprehensive in that it builds on things that are already working—and will bring cohesion to the many different efforts that are going on—as well as explores other strategies for success. It involves students, parents and staff.

APRIL 10

The girls' basketball team brought home the gold today. We had some of our students attend the game to cheer them on. It was a great team effort. I am so impressed with the job our coaches do with our students.

We have two girls who, when they came to Lawrence Heights in grade 6, I could see they would be unstoppable by the time they reached grade 8. That proved to be correct as they were both outstanding members of the team. I was pleased to see our grade 6 and 7 students also played a key role—cheers!

As we begin planning for next year I have asked that preference forms to be returned to the office today. The forms give me an idea of which responsibilities staff members would like to be included in or excluded from next year. It is important to me that we provide opportunities for staff to contribute in the areas they feel comfortable with and have expertise in.

APRIL 11

The Sandy saga continues. Today she arrived at school at 9:30 and refused to go to class. She said she wouldn't go to a class with people who got her brother arrested. After a whole lot of counselling and encouragement aimed at helping her identify the right decision, she decided that she wanted a transfer and left the school.

A short time later I get a call from her mother who wants an explanation of what has happened. She replies by saying she is not going to let her daughter—who has now arrived at home and is banging on the door—in the house. She is fed up and disgusted with Sandy's behaviour. Sandy then decides to call the police. They respond by picking her up and bringing her back to school and calling Children's Aid.

Children's Aid is familiar with the student as they have had some concerns about Sandy since 1993, but they think this is an attendance issue, which they don't have a role in resolving. We also contact our attendance counsellor, who has been notified on several occasions about this particular student. He offers to get her into an alternative school, but Sandy refuses.

Her presence continues to make a negative impact on the rest of our student body and thus we have no choice but to suspend her for persistent opposition to authority.

APRIL 13

Today we host the Math Olympics at our school. It is a great event that is congruent with the kind of messages we are trying to give our students. The teams entered from our school represented us well and everyone in attendance has a great day of problem solving and learning.

The event has made me reflect further on the challenge of equity of educational opportunity. Because, if educators only reacted and were not proactive, then only one (cultural) group would be represented on our team, and our staff all had a problem with that. So we asked our staff to get involved with the recruiting of math team members particularly from groups that are underrepresented. We have to remember that equity means equal access to the benefits that an educational system has to offer, and that this may require differential treatment.

I have worked with many teachers who want to prepare all students for a future that is commensurate with their abilities and desires. These teachers are aware of the statistics that show that many students of colour and females are not pursuing mathematics and science as careers. Achievement and participation by these students, in my opinion, is impeded by societal stereotypes. We, as educators, must first understand that these stereotypes exist and then recognize that we contribute to them both voluntarily and involuntarily.

Our actions and the actions of society make students of colour and female students vulnerable to race and gender biases. These students bear the societal labels that are associated with their groups. Society in general sees female students as strong in the arts and social sciences but weak and uninterested in technical areas. Society views students of colour as deficit and in need of remediation. These students are vulnerable because very often they accept the definitions of an unjust educational process. As a result, they don't recognize that they are being marginalized, or identify with an appropriate educational process, and learning does not take place as it should.

We have to understand that the government cannot legislate the changes that need to take place in our classrooms. We must be willing to go through personal changes that ensure equitable academic opportunities are provided to all students. These changes will require that we consider such things as teacher interactions with students, teacher pre-service and in-service training, academic groupings of students, learning styles of students, and remediation versus acceleration as it concerns student achievement.

Later in the evening we took sixty students from our school and twenty from our feeder schools to the YTV Achievement Awards. It was a special evening honouring Canada's young people. The students particularly liked the musical performance of teen sensation Sammie. It was a late evening but certainly worth it.

APRIL 14

The feedback about the YTV Awards from our students was most insightful. Although they thoroughly enjoyed the show, they were concerned with the lack of visible minority youth among those being honoured. They went so far as to check the YTV website to confirm their suspicions and they were correct. The only Black youth honoured was a breakdancer.

APRIL 15

The Saturday School Program kicked off the second session, which will go until to the end of the school year. Forty something students showed up to sharpen their literacy and technology skills.

Our choir members received royal treatment at the Harry Jerome Awards. They had their own dressing rooms (one for the girls and one for the boys) and were treated to dinner before their performance. They were obviously feeling pretty good as they delivered an outstanding performance under the direction of Dr. Marine, and they received a standing ovation.

APRIL 17

Our grade 6 team of teachers attended a workshop on the EQAO preparation, and spent the rest of the day planning for the testing set to begin May 17. All grade 6 students congregated in the cafeteria to receive a pep talk about the EQAO and to start their preparations.

Our staff committee held its first meeting to determine the priorities for the upcoming school year. Unfortunately we are going to have to replace some outstanding teachers who will be moving on.

APRIL 18

A focus group discussion with student representatives from every class has been revealing. The students were given the task of brainstorming what they like about Lawrence Heights and what needs to improve. Student feedback was also used to gain further information on student perception.

The things our students like about the school are the opportunities and the relationships they have with staff. What they don't like is the sometimes rampant disrespect demonstrated by their peers. They also don't like what appear to be second, third and fourth chances given to students who don't meet the school's expectations. Surprisingly enough the progress reports were seen as a positive.

APRIL 19

Our trustee visited the school today. She has been a big supporter of our school and drops in on occasion to visit. Today I present her with a copy of our National Quality Institute submission and a "Believing in Achieving" T-shirt. We engage in some intriguing discussions, which always end up in a discussion about what is good for our students.

APRIL 20

Today is the anniversary of the Columbine school shooting, where fourteen students and a teacher were fatally shot at school by students. All of us in school settings are a little on edge in spite of statistics which show that young people are much more likely to be shot and killed on the street or at home than in school.

But then last Thursday a teenager at a high school in Ottawa injured four students when he stabbed them, himself and an adult with a steak knife. And this was at a school thought to be in a "good" neighbourhood and populated by "good" kids. I think we all need to realize this is not a school problem, or a social services problem, or a police problem. This is a community problem.

Many observers have said the problem is access to guns, and video games and music lyrics that contribute to these tragedies. I have always believed that music, games and guns don't kill people, people do—so what are we doing about that? By all accounts the Columbine killers and the Ottawa teen were misfits and became the victims of practical jokes. After the incidents no one said, "What a surprise. They were good students." Everyone said, "It figures."

The National School Safety Centre in the United States has compiled a list of signs common to potentially violent teens. These include recognizing those who: 1) have a history of tantrums and uncontrollable outbursts, 2) habitually make violent threats, 3) are often depressed and/or have significant mood swings, 4) have been bullied or have bullied or intimidated peers or younger children.

We end the short week on an upbeat note with a basketball competition in the morning and a dance in the afternoon. Students also receive a progress report on their way home. It is the long weekend and many of us will be celebrating Easter or Passover.

APRIL 25

My morning starts with a leadership team meeting, which is much more than I expected as a motivational speaker is our guest. It was refreshing and thought provoking to hear Dick O'Brien speak about the ten fundamental principles for reducing stress in our lives—the timing couldn't have been better.

The Journey of Life (95% of the stress in your life is self induced)
- Do not exaggerate the negative in your life.
- Do not replay bad experiences over and over again.
- Choose to function with a resilient attitude whenever possible.
- Learn to break out of your reactive modes.
- Be aware of the quality of your own self-talk.
- Learn to create positive images in your mind when you face new challenges.
- Learn to let things go.
- Eat right, sleep and get regular exercise.
- Take ownership of your day and your life before you leave home.
- Never lose your sense of humour (O'Brien 2000).

APRIL 26

Today is secretary's day and a time in which we give thanks to our secretaries. They really are so much more than their title reveals and are such a big part of all we do here at Lawrence. They counsel, they administer first aid, they lend an ear to staff and they so wonderfully represent the spirit of Lawrence Heights in their daily interactions with staff, students and community—THANKS!

Our EQAO preparations continue with a parent information night. Once again we have a significant turn out, but I am still feeling somewhat disappointed that some of the parents who really need to be here aren't. It seems that we are preaching to the converted.

On my way out of the meeting, I am stopped by a parent who is very interested in doing whatever he can to help his daughter succeed. He has offered to pay for a tutor and anything else that will ensure her success. His daughter is a level 4 (A student) and will be fine.

APRIL 27

I spent the morning at one of the local high schools as a presenter in their career fair. They asked me to come and talk about my experience as a former professional athlete. I brought four students along with me who are outstanding athletes but need to do more in the classroom. I shared some of my experiences as a student athlete and my experiences as a professional.

The Kevin Ross story certainly captured their interest because it debates the value of sports, particularly to the Black student athlete, and asks the question, what happens to Black student athletes once their athletic career ends? Do their stories read like Kevin Ross's or do they read like Thomas LaVeist?

Kevin Ross was a basketball player at Creighton University in Omaha. Ross spent four years at Creighton as a member of the basketball team and a member of the student body. However, after his athletic eligibility was exhausted and he was unable to succeed with an NBA team, he found himself a functional illiterate with only seventy credit hours of college course work. He made headlines by enrolling in the Marva Collins Westside Preparatory School in Chicago, beginning as a fifth grader. At present Kevin Ross is suing Creighton University.

Thomas LaVeist grew up in a tough section of Brooklyn. Although very intelligent, LaVeist never truly applied himself during his high school days. He was a student with "A" ability, but he performed at "C" level. He was fortunate enough to receive a football scholarship from the University of Maryland-Eastern Shore. While at UMES, LaVeist became a more diligent student. He went on to receive a PhD in medical sociology. Today, Dr. Thomas LaVeist is a very successful professor at Johns Hopkins University School of Public Health in Maryland, as well as the president of the Alexandria

Consortium, a prominent consulting firm. Dr. LaVeist credits much of his success to the educational opportunity he received. Because of his poor high school academic record, and his family's financial situation, he would never have been able to go to college without an athletic scholarship.

A reporter from *Reader's Digest* was in the school today doing some research on a possible story about our school. The student ambassadors carried the day by giving her an extensive tour of the school, screening our school video and running a PowerPoint presentation. She also got a tour of the community and a visit to the local high school courtesy of our guidance counsellor.

April 30

A former student, Corrina, arrives at our doorstep crying and very upset. I invite her into the office only to learn she has run away from school and home. She is feeling lonely and afraid in her new surroundings and needs the comfort of our school. She has recently moved for the third time in the last five months. After some time counselling and talking with her we agree to let her stay for the day, provide her with some lunch and bus tickets to get home. We come to the decision after we have spoken to her parent and the principal of her school to let them know her concerns and that she is safe.

May 3

Is parent involvement a valuable, if largely untapped, resource for schools struggling with diminishing funds? A way to instill pride and interest in schooling. A way to increase student achievement and enhance a sense of community and commitment? Uh, let me think about it—YES! No question. But there are some who view it as one more responsibility to add to overburdened teachers and administrators—or even as a threat to the autonomy and professionalism of the schools.

As a school we have failed. Failed to get parents to support their children's schooling by attending school functions and responding to school obligations (parent-teacher conferences for example). We know that they can become more involved in helping their children improve their school work by providing encouragement, arranging for appropriate study time and space, modelling desired behaviour (such as reading for pleasure), monitoring homework and actively tutoring their children at home.

Research overwhelmingly demonstrates that parent involvement in children's learning is positively related to achievement. Further, the research shows that the more intensively parents are involved in their children's learning, the more beneficial are the achievement effects. Looking more closely at the research, there are strong indications that the most effective forms of parent involvement are those which engage parents in working directly with their children on learning activities at home. Programs that involve parents in reading with their children, supporting their work on homework assignments, or tutoring them using materials and instructions provided by teachers, show particularly impressive results.

Along similar lines, researchers have found that the more active forms of parent involvement produce greater achievement benefits than the passive ones. That is, if parents receive phone calls, read and sign written communications from the school, and perhaps attend and listen during parent–teacher conferences, greater achievement benefits accrue than would be the case with no parent involvement at all. However, considerably greater achievement benefits are noted when parent involvement is active (when parents work with their children at home, certainly, but also when they attend and actively support school activities and when they help out in classrooms or on field trips, and so.

The research also shows that the earlier in a child's educational process parent involvement begins, the more powerful the effects will be. Educators frequently point out the critical role of the home and family environment in determining children's school success, and it appears that the earlier this influence is harnessed, the greater the likelihood of higher student achievement. Early childhood education programs with strong parent involvement components have amply demonstrated the effectiveness of this approach.

Contrary to what many have said, parents from disadvantaged backgrounds can and do make a positive contribution to their children's achievement in school if they receive adequate training and encouragement in the types of parent involvement that can make a difference. Even more significant, the research dispels a popular myth by revealing that parents can make a difference regardless of their own levels of education. Indeed, disadvantaged children have the most to gain from parent involvement programs.

Because of the special problems and the potential associated with disadvantaged parent involvement, care must be taken to emphasize the concept of parents as partners of the school. Too often, because of the distance between teachers/administrators and the communities in which our schools are located, school staff can tend to view the parents and surrounding community as needing to change and having little to offer. This deficit model is clearly detrimental to the development of positive attitudes about education and good working relationships between the community and the school.

With the EQAO rapidly approaching and other year-end testing for our grade 7 and 8 students, I am still concerned with what seems to me to be a lack of the love of learning. It is something that I have addressed with our student body a number times. I have provided examples and opportu-

Dear Parent(s) Guardian(s):

Student achievement is the key focus of everything that we do at Lawrence Heights. We hold tenaciously to the view that all students, with no exceptions and no excuses, must be held to high expectations of academic progress, and that skilled and knowledgeable instruction can assist all students—from the high achiever to the child with specific needs—to meet the challenge within the context of his or her individual life.

There has been progress, but not nearly enough. Recognizing that literacy is the initial key to improve student achievement across the board, we have developed specific grade frameworks to promote quality literacy instruction in our classrooms.

Students need to be engaged in their schoolwork. This can be measured by the amount of time they devote to their academics and the intensity with which they work. We must demand extra effort from our students and continue to provide support for them, recognizing that not all students achieve at the same rate. These supports have included lengthening the school day and the school year by providing summer school at Lawrence, and a Saturday School Program.

Schools cannot make the changes alone. Parents have a crucial role to play in helping to improve student achievement. The parents of this community must step further forward to become active participants in their children's education. The result we seek is a stronger home/school partnership to support teaching and learning in the classroom. We simply do not have at the present time an acceptable level of parent participation at Lawrence Heights. Our teachers cannot and must not be left to do it alone.

I trust that the Lawrence Heights community recognizes that the initiatives we have undertaken throughout the year are pivotal to our collective efforts to improve learning. This is and shall remain a journey, not a destination, filled with challenges and the greatest of rewards.

I am confident that the course we are on will result, over time, in steady progress, measured by increased success and enhanced opportunity for our students.

Sincerely,

Chris Spence
Principal

nities for students to change their attitudes. I understand that it won't happen overnight, but we have to continually focus our students on what really matters and that is a love of learning. I have often said that if we as a school took our academics as seriously as we do our social events, we would all be on the honour roll. Now don't get me wrong, I fully understand the age group that we service and all that they are dealing with, but here we try to emphasize a balance in our lives, with the focus on academics. Part of our role is to prepare our students for what they will face in high school and beyond, and we all know this preparation starts in the classroom. When I stop a student in the hall and she tells me she does the work, I say, don't just do it, accomplish your work, otherwise it is just activity. To try to increase parental support, I wrote a latter and sent it home with the students.

MAY 8

Our grade 7 students left for Shadow Lake today and will be gone for the week. It is noticeably quiet around the school with them gone. The outdoor education experience is a great one for the students. This will be their second visit.

MAY 9

Human rights are fundamental inalienable rights claimed by virtue of being human. They are the essentials to which we are entitled to preserve the integrity and dignity of life. By examining these issues in schools, students can acquire not only the knowledge, but also the skills and attitudes necessary in a democracy. Thus human rights education is an essential part that should infuse every facet of the curriculum.

Martin Luther King once said that injustice anywhere is a threat to justice everywhere. In our schools we need to raise awareness of human rights conditions around the world; to promote understanding of the forces that create these conditions around the world and those which can change them; and to encourage action rooted in a humane conception of justice and human dignity. We are pleased to have a retired principal visit the school today and give us a presentation on a worthwhile cause he has been involved with called Sleeping Children Around The World. The organization raises funds to provide bed kits to the children who will benefit the most in underdeveloped and developing countries.

Sleeping Children Around The World is the brainchild of Murray Dryden, who had a few sleepless nights of his own during the Depression. He feels that the comfort of a bed is a basic right of every child and that there is nothing more peaceful than a sleeping child.

This is certainly something we as a school will get involved with, as it gives our students the opportunity to give back and be sensitive to the needs of others. We agree to host some fundraisers to raise enough money to buy ten bed kits. Our student council has done a terrific job of fundraising all year—and what a great cause this one is.

Later in the afternoon I meet with our superintendent and Dana Flemington, the principal of our feeder school, to discuss the National Quality Institute's visit on June 5. Flemington won the award last year and the staff have been very helpful in our preparations.

MAY 10

Over the next two days our students will be involved in the District Track and Field Championships. We always field a strong team and I suspect this year won't be any different. All students who are participating know they must be meeting the academic and social expectations of the school.

I am thrilled to hear one of our students won the boys' one hundred meter final. It is especially gratifying for him because he is a terrific athlete who had to sit out the basketball season because of his academics.

MAY 11

Our students did well at the Track and Field Championship, finishing third overall. Congratulations to the students and staff. I call the young man who won the one hundred meters to the office to personally congratulate him and I call his father and let him know as well. As I told the young man, it is a pleasure to make this phone call home because there have been far too many calls to his home that have not been positive.

The good, the bad and the ugly—that is the only way to describe Bill 69 (the Education Accountability Act) introduced in the legislature yesterday. The Act passed first reading and has the following four general components:

The Good
Establishment of new average class sizes: currently, the number of secondary students per teacher is twenty-two. This will be reduced to twenty-one. Currently, the average number of elementary students per teacher is twenty-five. This will be reduced to twenty-four and twenty-four and a half for elementary overall.

The Bad
Addressing instructional time: the legislation will require secondary school teachers to increase their workload and carry an average of at least 6.6 eligible courses. This legislation will ensure that school boards and teachers' unions meet this requirement.

Co-instructional activities: this legislation will require that each school board develop a plan to provide co-instructional (before and after school) activities for students.

The Ugly
Compliance with board obligations in more than financial areas: the Minister of Education has the right to investigate and offer binding direction to boards of education if a board was to make a motion to break the law or consider breaking the law.

The concept of quality education appears to be secondary to who has the power and who is going to run the show. Unfortunately, it is the students who become the victims.

MAY 12

I was invited to speak at the Equity Conference at York University today. The title of my presentation is SkinGames and focuses on balancing academics and athletics, which continues to be problematic for Black student athletes.

Many of the participants share their stories of failure and low expectations of Black student athletes.

MAY 15

Today we start our school-wide vision sharing. We have asked all students to create a two or three sentence vision of where they are going in life. I am absolutely convinced that by articulating and sharing their vision they become accountable for their learning and behaviour each and every time they walk through the front doors. It really gives meaning to why they come to school and emphasizes that, no matter what they want to do in life, in all likelihood it starts in the classroom. From now until the end of the school year students will be stopped periodically and asked to share their vision. It really is a necessary exercise as one student replied:

"Whadda ya mean, future?"

"What do you think you want to be doing, say in five years?" I asked.

"What's up with that? My future is right now. To get as much as I can—RIGHT NOW."

"Why?"

"We all know we aren't gonna make twenty-one. There's no hope here. None. It makes no difference what we do, or what you do. The only hope for people here is to leave and never come back."

MAY 29

Representatives from Gatorade will be visiting our school this week and putting our students through a fitness test and talking about dehydration. I think it is important that our students get plenty of opportunities to realize the importance of fitness and physical exercise. It really is a lifestyle choice that we can play a key role in developing. I am particularly concerned with young women who the older they get the more likely they are to opt out of physical education classes, even though the research says there are significant physical and psychological benefits to sport participation. Young women who play sports are more confident, have higher levels of self-esteem and stronger self-concepts. They are more likely to graduate from high school and less likely to get involved with drugs or get pregnant. As little as four hours of exercise a week reduces a woman's risk of breast cancer by almost 60 percent, an affliction that affects one out of every eight women in our society. Sports are where boys traditionally learn teamwork, goal setting and the pursuit of excellence in performance—critical skills necessary for success in the workplace. To maintain a healthy lifestyle in an economic environment where the quality of our children's lives will depend on their ability to earn two incomes in a household, our daughters need to be as prepared for the highly competitive workplace as our sons.

The first day is a huge success. The students love it and the Gatorade representatives strike an instant rapport with our students.

MAY 30

Fifty of our grade 6 students visit the University of Toronto today. It is a great opportunity for them to be exposed to an institution of higher learning. We are fortunate to have a productive and lasting relationship with the U of T. The university provides the opportunity for some of our students to receive a summer scholarship to attend science and math camp.

Our first and second year teachers will have the opportunity to attend a presentation by Barbara Colorossa, a well known speaker on issues related to children. The opportunity is being provided by our superintendent as part of her plan to address issues of staff morale, which has been a big issue since Bill 160.

I think all educators are reeling from the Bill, which seems to say so little about quality education. At the heart of the debate is the *Education Quality Improvement Act*, which essentially is about structures, power and collective bargaining. It is about who can set taxes or determine class sizes, basically who will run the show. Many of us fear that this could eventually result in a totally different kind of education system based on the market approach of competition. I for one am not convinced that this strategy will solve the problems in our schools which have a significant population of disadvantaged students. In fact, it will exacerbate the problems. The only way to improve the schools serving disadvantaged students is to develop policies that directly address the educational challenges that these schools face.

Charter schools, which are independent public schools, are designed and operated by educators, parents, community leaders and others. Attendance in these schools is by choice; thus they are held to the highest level of accountability—consumer demand.

Advocates for charter schools share a belief that if schools had to compete for students the quality of education would improve. The problem is that not all schools compete on a level playing field. Usually, schools with high proportions of European or white and privileged students are considered "good" schools by the majority in Canada. Those with high proportions of minorities or disadvantaged students are considered less desirable, and therefore start the competition significantly disadvantaged. This in effect leaves the "good" schools free to select students they wish to select, which will probably, more often than not, be students who are easy to teach, while the "not so good" schools will have to accept anyone who comes along.

Voucher programs are another step down the path toward more choice and competition. This program proposes the distribution of monetary vouchers to parents of school-aged children, usually in disadvantaged areas. Parents could use the vouchers toward the cost of tuition at private schools. To me this type of program sends a clear message that we are giving up on public education, which is founded on inclusiveness.

MAY 31

The grade 5 students who will join us next school year visited the school today as part of our transition program. We planned an exciting day for them that ended with a pizza lunch. I am somewhat disappointed that Nester, one of the top students from one of our feeder schools, is shopping around for schools as he has some concerns about our school. His sister has had a brilliant stay at Lawrence Heights. His sister passed on this information to me, so I asked her to get her brother to drop by the school again sometime.

JUNE 1

Now that we have completed our hiring process for next year, many questions have been raised about who is appropriate to teach whom and who is appropriate to teach what. In these times there is an increased emphasis on diversity within our educational communities. Although the percentage of minority group students is increasing, the percentage of minority teachers is decreasing. Some efforts to attract minority group members to the teaching profession are already underway, and more should be undertaken. The limited research in this area indicates that higher percentages of minority teachers in schools are beneficial to all students.

The relationship between the minority teacher population and minority student performance is complex and will not be analyzed in detail here. While no claims are made that minority students have to be taught by minority teachers in order to learn well, it seems that there are definite benefits to having plenty of minority group teachers in largely minority group schools, or any school for that matter.

The National Association of Scholars argues that entertaining the question of who can teach whom unnecessarily politicizes the academy. They argue that academic freedom is based on disciplinary competence and entails a responsibility to exclude extraneous political matters from the classroom (Short 1988: 7). Thus, in their minds, a teacher's gender, class, sexual orientation and race do not have an effect on a teacher's approach to teaching; only one's competence matters.

However, studies have shown that in addition to competence and enthusiasm, a teacher's personal characteristics do have an effect on the teaching process for some students (United States Department of Education 1990). Most often, these are the same students who tend to be marginalized by the educational system.

Today's students increasingly come from diverse backgrounds and bring a wide range of needs, expectations, identities and beliefs to school. As educators we must pay attention to these differences and seek to understand the experiences of diverse groups if we are going to be able to build multicultural schools in the future. Attention to these dynamics allows for the development of rapport, which is a necessity for effective teaching (United States Department of Education 1990). If we cannot communicate, we cannot teach or learn. If students' and teachers' worlds are galaxies apart, prospects are poor for effective instruction (Short 1988). Lack of identification with teachers by students of colour, and by lesbian, bisexual, gay and female students often leads them to feel under appreciated, discouraged, disenfranchised and alienated.

Nester, the young man who is shopping around for schools, visits the school today and we have an excellent meeting. What an impressive young man—clearly he is going somewhere in his life. He expresses to me his concerns around the focus of the school; he believes and has heard it is not on academics and safety. Rumours of bullying and extortion continue to plague the reputation of our school. I address all his concerns and ask him to speak with his sister and to visit the other schools he is considering. I assure him that I am confident we can compete with any of them.

Tom then takes Nester on a tour of the school and engages in some conversation, which reveals that his teacher actually encouraged him to go elsewhere. My disappointment is evident and I call Dana, the principal of the school, who is shocked to hear this. We have, I think, an excellent working relationship with all of our feeder schools.

Tonight is our last School Council meeting of the year and we have another strong turnout (thirty-three parents). We take some time to review the year and do a start, stop and continue evaluation—where the principal and vice-principal get feedback from students about the school.

I spend some time reviewing parent responses before leaving to go home—the results are outstanding. We continue to have an extraordinary approval rating from our community. They refer to the continuation of summer and Saturday school and the extended opportunities for students to develop self-esteem.

JUNE 2

Today is the deadline for summer scholarships. It has become a part of our tradition here at Lawrence Heights to provide students with the opportunity to attend a summer camp on a scholarship. Last year we sent more than thirty students to various camps such as art, music, computers, basketball, soccer, science and track and field. This year students have to apply for the opportunity to go, and parents have to commit to ensuring their son or daughter arrives at the camp for its entire duration. We had some difficulties around that last year. Students who didn't show up left us in a position where we had to pay the school fee ahead of time to guarantee a spot.

I was invited to speak at York University faculty of education. It turned out to be a wonderful experience as the audience is a group of educators from Kuwait. They were most interested in some of the programs and philosophies of our school, but were intrigued with the school's promotional video, "Living the Dream," which had them laughing and crying with tears of joy. I promised to send them a copy of the video.

JUNE 5

Today is the day the National Quality Institute comes to our school to do a site visit. I arrive at school much earlier than usual to ensure all looks well, and it does—the school looks fabulous.

As I walk around the school I drop in on the badminton club tournament, which is just underway in the gym. This is the first year for the tournament. Badminton is a sport that our students need further exposure to and opportunity to play.

A team of five assessors will conduct focus groups to determine the merits of our submission, which is truly something to behold. The presentation of the submission and its contents really are outstanding. Thanks to all staff members who had a hand in the submission for their tireless efforts. Students and staff are both anxious and excited about the day; we have been anticipating this day for the last couple of weeks.

The assessors meet with our senior management group: our superintendent, principal, vice principals and convenors. The meeting is intense and lasts for more than two hours with direct questioning around the table about the school and the quality principles.

The next two focus groups involve a cross-section of staff including office staff, cafeteria staff, caretaking staff, support staff and teaching staff. All in attendance are feeling positive about their meeting.

The day ends with our students giving the assessors a tour of the school, watching the school video with them and running a PowerPoint presentation done by students. All in all the day was a success. Now we have to sit and wait for the results, which will be released sometime in August.

Scheduled visits by Covenant House and Katherine from the Marvellettes are also happening in the school today. We have done some fundraising for Covenant House and this is a follow up to that. Today they will meet with the grade 8 students.

Katherine of the Marvellettes has become connected to our school. We met her when the choir visited and performed at the Motown Museum in Detroit, and ever since she has made regular phone calls and the occasional visit to the school. Once again our guidance counsellor, Tom, has been instrumental in initiating a relationship that benefits our students in many ways. For example, our students have interviewed many of the legends of Motown via phone conversations. The students who are participating are required to research the artist, then develop some question, do and summarize the interview, and share the results with their peers. Because it is something they want to do, they don't see it as work, but along the way they are developing useful skills. Just the other day when I returned to the school from a meeting and went to my office I was politely greeted by a student who asked me to hush and hoped it was okay that they were in my office using the phone to interview Motown legend Martha Reeves from the Vandellas.

JUNE 6

You could sense a sigh of relief in the school today. Yesterday was pretty intense, but we all felt very positive about it. Students and staff have been inquiring all day wondering how we did with the National Quality Institute visit. There is such a sense of pride, accomplishment and confidence in the air. As one student said, "Dr. Spence, just look at the school and what we've accomplished. They would be crazy not to give us that award."

JUNE 7

Next year we are going to get the opportunity to be a host school for teacher candidates from the faculty of education at York University. The students will be coming from the fine arts program. This will give us an opportunity to learn from their expertise in an area that our school continues to develop and to provide them with a supportive learning environment. The coordinator of the program and I have an upbeat meeting that leaves us both excited abut the possibilities.

JUNE 8

The day gets off to a rocky start when an irate parent visits the school because she thinks her daughter is being picked on. The student, Samantha, has had significant difficulty meeting the expectations of the school and is more often than not flat out rude and disrespectful when conversing with her teachers. But as per usual, by the time the story reaches home the story has changed significantly. I am taken aback when the mother suggests the reason her daughter gets sent home is because she is white—a comment that I don't take lightly. Samantha is visibly upset that her mother would play the race card and denies ever making such an accusation. The plot thickens when I ask two of the student's teachers to join us in the meeting. It just so happens that the two teachers that spend the most time teaching the student are white. There is nothing like concrete examples to put a fire out, and that is exactly what the teachers provide. The meeting ends on a positive note and Samantha's mother apologizes for some of her comments. She too agrees that in order to get respect you have to give it; this is something her daughter has not done on a regular basis. As the parent is leaving the school I remind her of the success her son is having at the school and the summer scholarship he is receiving in the arts.

A teacher from one of our feeder schools shows up today to apologize for what she thinks is a misinterpretation of something she said. This goes back to Nester, the student who was shopping around for another school after his teacher had apparently subtly encouraged him to do so. I could see that she was feeling guilty about the situation and she did her best to make amends. She explained to me what she had said and how this bright young man may have misinterpreted her comments. Anyway the bottom line is he's coming to Lawrence Heights and we think he made the right choice.

It is the time of year when lots of activities are going on inside and outside of the school. Today, a group of students and staff are going to Rocky Ridge Ranch to do some horseback riding and to learn how to groom a horse. Tomorrow we are off to Ontario Place.

JUNE 9

I return to the school to find out about a disturbing phone call that took place yesterday. A student apparently went home and told his father that a staff member had grabbed him on his way out of the building. The father consequently called the school in a somewhat threatening manner. Our vice-principal was able to calm him down by assuring him that we will investigate the allegations. We investigate first thing in the morning only to find out that what was referred to as being grabbed was merely a tap on the shoulder. I call the father immediately to relay the findings and he is calm and collected. He listens and is responsive. We engage in a discussion about the school and he is critical of a number of things, including what he perceives to be an overemphasis on Black culture.

I find myself explaining why Black History month is devoted to educating everyone about the accomplishments of African Canadians/Americans who helped to shape this country. It serves to highlight heroes who often are overlooked when history books are written. The parent thinks it may be difficult for others to be involved in what appears to be something created only for African Canadians/Americans. Sometimes recognizing cultural diversity becomes confused with creating more racial divisions. Students might feel resentful that there is no white history month.

These statements, however, miss the point. If white students feel out of place learning about prominent African Canadians/Americans, they become more attuned to how Black students feel in most history classes that focus primarily on white males. Black History Month is not just another way to segregate history into white and black sections. Hopefully, by highlighting important Black issues and accomplishments and figures during February and beyond, these facts can become a part of the history curriculum. Our society needs this reminder every year. Undeniable racial lines still exist, despite the best efforts of many. Anyway, I do more listening than anything as the parent vents his frustration about being white and living in a predominantly Black area.

One of our students has been bringing a kitten to school for the last couple of days and, as cute as the kitten is, it needs to be at home. When we call the student's home his parent knows nothing about the kitten. Apparently the student has been hiding the kitten in a gym bag that he got from a neighbour. He was afraid that he wouldn't be able to keep the kitten, but the situation quickly turns into a trust issue even though the student was well intentioned.

JUNE 12

Approximately 90 percent of the issues we deal with when students are sent to the office are about a lack of respect. Today all staff will be introduced to the Tribes process (Gibbs 1998). The purpose of the Tribes process is to assure the healthy development of every student so that each has the knowledge, skills and resiliency to be successful in a rapidly changing world. Tribes is not a curriculum. It is a process that develops inclusion, influence and community. Academic material is taught through cooperative learning strategies.

Our grade 8 students will be involved in an HIV presentation given by the Lawrence Heights Community Health Centre. It is certainly an issue that warrants discussion—so much so that I wrote and produced a twenty-four-minute drama to address the issue.

"Teammates" is a screenplay written in response to the fight against HIV and AIDS. Even the massive amount of media publicity around this largely sexually transmitted disease has not fully convinced a large number of youth to change their sexual lifestyle. The fact is, there continues to be a homophobic attitude and an ongoing belief that HIV/AIDS is a gay male disease.

A needs assessment (Spence 1996) revealed that AIDS education is still a tough sell, even though it's literally a matter of life and death. A recent report (Hawkins 1994) found that HIV, the virus that causes AIDS, is spreading unchecked among adolescents regardless of where they live or their economic status.

The film revolves around Marcus Thompson, an eighteen-year-old first-year university student on an athletic scholarship. Marcus has everything going for him: a promising academic and basketball career, a loving and supportive family, a beautiful girlfriend, an adoring brother and a community that considers him to be their home town hero. His life is shattered when he discovers he is HIV positive after a casual sexual encounter with a classmate, Vanessa Adams. The story examines the young man's and woman's struggle to come to terms with the fact that they now have HIV, and how they try to put their lives back together with the support of family and friends.

JUNE 13

Our choir has been taking a break lately in order to focus on academic testing over the last couple of months. It is amazing how many opportunities to perform we have been given. Today we hit the road to perform at the University of Toronto. Ben and Jerry's Ice Cream is launching some new flavours and has asked us to perform. Once again the choir doesn't disappoint—an outstanding performance leaves the audience smiling.

Soccer season is here and we have three teams that will compete in a district tournament over the next couple of days.

Tonight after school we will host a math workshop focused on measurement. We have let our staff know that we expect a strong Lawrence Heights presence.

JUNE 14

Interest in the Learning Equation continues to be expressed around the province, and we at Lawrence Heights continue to open our doors for educators who wish to observe the program in operation with students. One class in particular has taken this demonstration role on. This responsibility has become a source of pride and accomplishment for this class. The students and teacher love it. It is quite wonderful to drop into the lab while they are doing the program and listen to them explain to visitors what they are doing. As you know, when you teach you learn.

JUNE 17

It's Saturday and here we are at school. We are hosting a lawn sale and barbecue at the school with live music and a car wash. A staff member's father used to own a dollar store and has donated a ton of great stuff to us to sell as part of the fundraiser to support student programs and field trips. Although the turnout is not great we have a heck of a good time. The live music played by staff, students, our audiovisual technician and a friend of his is great fun.

JUNE 19

Our school-wide science fair has become a great opportunity for our students to showcase their talents. This year is no different. A strong showing among the winners by the girls in the school is particularly rewarding. The staff who organize the event are to be congratulated for their time and effort. The only disappointment is the poor turnout by the community. This has been become a constant theme—they just don't know what they are missing.

Project Sci-FFem is a program that I want to get up and going to meet the needs of our girls in science. Sci-FFem stands for science for females. It would be a full-time gifted program for grade 7 girls that would provide hands-on science learning. There is a need to encourage more females to pursue careers in science. Research suggests that parent and teacher attitudes, group dynamics in the classroom and choices made by girls themselves all contribute to less participation in science by girls than boys (Eccles 1987).

JUNE 20

After last year I just wasn't sure if we as a school should go through with a talent show again this year. It became very disruptive for the school, as students were asking to leave class to rehearse because we have two different lunch hours, one for grades 6 and 7 and another for grade 8. If you had someone in your group who didn't share the same lunch hour it became a problem. Then there were difficulties around staff coverage. It seemed like every student was a part of some group that needed staff coverage and a room to practice in. If only we as a school took our academics as seriously as the talent show. Nonetheless the students love it, and it is one more opportunity for them to showcase some of their talents. This year's show is somewhat disappointing only because the same organizational problems have come into play. Again it is very disruptive for the rest of the school and I have to address the staff's concerns at an assembly. The situation is exemplified when a group wants to perform a song in which the lyrics are disgusting. They are canned from the show but to my amazement they don't understand why!

We decide that the show must go on but rehearsals are to take place at home, not the school. Our hand was forced when a fight almost erupted over the use of a room. The show turns out to be entertaining but short. A number of groups dropped out due to a lack of preparation and inappropriate material.

JUNE 21

Our grade 6 students are off to Wonderland today. They are going partially to play but mainly to learn. They will participate in Aboriginal Day celebrations.

The girls' soccer team won the gold medal today. We are very proud of them and the coaches. They worked hard and are as proud as can be with their gold medals.

JUNE 22

Today is the day that we say good-bye to our grade 8 students at our graduation ceremony. They really have progressed. They all look amazing dressed up with proud parents and family looking on. Noticeably absent is Sandy. We did meet with her mother and came up with a plan so that she could attend the graduation, but Sandy lost interest when we put some requirements in place.

JUNE 26

The last dance of the year is a great success with the students. We also hold a barbecue and give out free Popsicles.

Staff gather at our vice-principal's house for a get-together to end the year. It is nice to sit down with staff and reflect on a terrific year.

JUNE 27

The year-end awards assembly recognizes and celebrates all the outstanding achievements of students during the year. Plaques, medals, certificates and T-shirts are given out to successful students. We also have some student performances to keep the celebration lively.

Grade 6 students who have acheived level 4 receive their t-shirt.

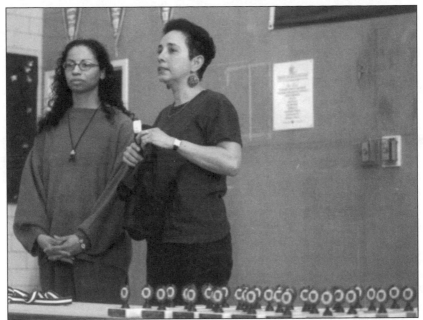

Our School Council chair Denise (left) receives her parent of the month award from our grade 6 convenor.

JUNE 28

Our final staff meeting is devoted to saying good-bye to the teachers who will be moving on.

Traditionally this has always been difficult. This year we are losing some who have been around for quite some time. Luckily, our guidance counsellor, who really adds a key ingredient to our school—HUMOUR—keeps us laughing, easing the pain. THANKS!

JUNE 29

It is only fitting that we send off our teachers who are leaving in style. A surprise assembly has been in the works for days and today is the day. With the help of our guidance counsellor, Tom, and our music teacher we invite each teacher up onto the stage to sing a rendition of "My Girl" to a rousing applause from the student body.

Then we present each departing teacher with a T-shirt, the same that we gave our celebrated students that says, "all yes—all year" in reference to our progress reports. The Sarah McLaughlin tune, "I Will Remember You," is dedicated to those teachers. Tears are flowing—it is a touching and memorable send off.

We end the assembly the same way we started, by having our Indian dancers, who are magnificent, perform. This time we ask the whole student body to stand and join in—what a celebration.

JUNE 30

Today we start to plan for next year. Team meetings and the opportunity to meet new staff are the order of the day. I also spend some time interviewing applicants for a position that just opened up. I think we have a keeper.

Conclusion: The Benefits of Effective Practices

Prominent effective schooling researchers—such as Edmonds (1977 and 1979a and b) and Levine and Lezotte (1990)—compare high-performing urban schools with schools that are demographically similar but have inferior student outcomes. These investigations lead them and other researchers to identify and list school and classroom factors that seem to make the difference between effective and ineffective schools. Effective schools, they report, are characterized by features such as strong administrative leadership focused on basic skills acquisition for all students; high expectations of students; teachers who take responsibility for their students' learning and adapt instruction to make sure that learning is taking place; safe and orderly school environments; the provision of incentives and rewards for student performance; and regular monitoring of student progress. The findings of the effective schooling researchers regarding the powerful effects of school-controllable variables have overturned the gloomy conclusions of early researchers. As stated by Soder and Andrews: "By identifying schools that were effective regardless of family income or ethnic status, the Effective Schools research ... attributed differences in children's performance to the schools themselves" (Soder and Andrews 1985: 8).

EFFECTIVE SCHOOLING PRACTICES

Strong administrative leadership

Administrators in effective schools give top priority to basic skills acquisition and are actively involved in helping to shape the instructional program. They support the instructional improvement efforts of teachers and provide the resources needed to make improvements possible.

Teacher responsibility and sense of self-efficacy

Effective teachers in urban schools servicing minority-group students see themselves as responsible for student learning. They do not perceive learning problems as products of students' personal backgrounds, but rather as indications that adaptations need to be made in their instructional approach so that learning can take place. These teachers believe in their ability to reach and teach virtually all of their students successfully (Edmonds 1977).

High expectations

Closely related to their belief in their own efficacy is these teachers' conviction that virtually all students can master basic learning objectives. Just as important, these teachers continually communicate these high expectations to students through their encouragement and support, and by holding students responsible for in-class participation, completing assignments and so forth. Since many students tend to interpret their scores or grades as purely a matter of luck or natural ability, these teachers emphasize to students the close relationship between personal effort and outcome (Northwest Regional Educational Laboratory 1990).

Safe, orderly, well-disciplined environments

Effective inner-city schools are characterized by school and classroom environments that are orderly and routine, but flexible. The school and classroom management literature underscores the need for rules and routines, but flexibility is also important. As Natriello, McDill and Pallas point out, hard and fast rules only work in settings where there aren't too many exceptional circumstances (Natriello, McDill and Pallas 1990). "The diversity and pressures in inner-city schools require flexible responses, especially regarding non-serious instructions" (Levine and Lezotte 1990: 2).

Teaching adapted to different student needs

As noted above, effective teachers are flexible in their teaching approaches. They recognize the need to modify and adapt instructional materials and methods to meet the needs of different students. They are aware of the personal and cultural learning style differences of their students and respond to these with appropriate teaching approaches.

Regular and frequent monitoring of student learning progress and provision of feedback

Successful teachers of urban minority students, like successful teachers of students in general, monitor students' progress closely so as to be able to adapt instruction as appropriate to meet learning needs. These teachers also are careful to keep students informed about their progress and about steps that will be taken to remediate any learning problems noted (Edmonds 1977 and 1979a and b; Levine and Lezotte 1990).

Staff development programs focused on school improvement

Effective schools will differ from less effective schools in that the former have strong staff development programs focused on school improvement. In addition, teachers in these schools have the power to influence the content and presentation of staff development activities (Northwest Laboratory 1991).

Use of school resources in support of priority goals

Decisions about the allocation of time, personnel, money and materials are made on the basis of which activities are most likely to further the school's priority goals. In effective schools, this usually means generous resource allocations to activities that can foster the development of reading, mathematics and language arts skills in all students (Edmonds 1977 and 1979a and b; Levine and Lezotte 1990).

Parent involvement

Research demonstrates that parent involvement in instruction, in support of classroom and extracurricular activities, and in school governance is related to positive student learning outcomes and attitudes. Research also shows that such involvement is especially beneficial for many minority children who may otherwise feel torn between the differing norms and values represented by the home and the school (Gursky 1990).

Use of cooperative learning structures

While students in general are often shown to benefit from cooperative learning structures. Some researchers note that cooperation is more in keeping with the cultural values of many Black students than is individual competition. In addition to the achievement benefits experienced by many students, cooperative learning has also been shown to enhance students' self-esteem, sense of self-efficacy as learners, cross-racial and cross-ethnic friendships, incidence of helping behaviour and empathy for others. (Knapp, Turnbull, and Shields 1990)

Peer and cross-age tutoring

Research has established that peer tutoring and cross-age tutoring arrangements are inexpensive and highly effective ways to build the basic reading and mathematics skills of young disadvantaged children so that the need for later remediation of skills deficits is reduced (Northwest Regional Educational Laboratory 1990).

Early childhood education programming

Research has amply demonstrated that inner-city children benefit enormously from Head Start and other forms of preschool programming, in terms of their later school achievement, attitudes, graduation rates and many other outcomes (Northwest Regional Educational Laboratory 1990).

Dividing large schools into smaller learning units and fostering ongoing relationships between students and school personnel

At the secondary level in particular, the academic performance of inner-city students is often hampered by feelings of alienation. This alienation is the result of large, impersonal schools and of structures in which students have few, if any, ongoing relationships with school staff members. Recent research has established that inner-city middle and high school students benefit when their schools are divided into smaller units where students and staff get to know one another and work together over longer periods of time than in traditional structures. In successful programs of this kind, teachers are frequently selected on the basis of their willingness and demonstrated ability to work with at-risk students.

Co-ordination of community resources

Inner-city students often have problems, such as health or nutrition needs, personal or family drug or alcohol problems, family abuse or neglect and so forth, that need to be addressed in order for teaching and learning to proceed successfully. Some inner-city programs have taken on the responsibility of coordinating an array of social services and other community resources to meet students' needs and these efforts have produced promising outcomes (Gursky 1990).

In addition to the importance of the effective schooling research findings for students, other more specific practices also enhance the quality of these young people's school experiences. To summarize, research indicates that the following elements enhance the achievement, attitudes and behaviour of minority group students:

- Strong leadership on the part of school administrators, which includes mobilizing resources to support the acquisition of basic skills by all students
- Teachers who believe they are responsible for students' learning and capable of teaching them effectively
- High expectations for student learning and behaviour on the part of administrators and teachers, and active communication of these expectations to students
- Safe, orderly, well-disciplined—but not rigid—school and classroom environments
- Teachers who are adept at modifying instructional materials and strategies in response to students' differing learning styles and needs.

The real issue has to do with finding solutions. We must all ask ourselves the question, what part of the solution can I play as a teacher, principal, educator, community member or parent? We all possess a piece of the solution. The challenge is to create the right school environment so that the discussions will result in solutions. Schools are very much the centre point of our communities. More than ever, what teachers do counts. No one is better positioned to engage the process of building hope.

It angers me when educators decide to go into teaching because summers are off or because they think it is an easy second income.

The Toronto District School Board is now attracting national attention because of its aggressive agenda that puts children first. I believe that we are on the right track and have laid the foundation for continuous progress. I salute, with great respect and admiration, the scores of dedicated educators and staff members who work tirelessly on behalf of our students. I thank the many parents, community and business members who have offered their unwavering support, encouragement, resources and expertise.

Deciding to go into teaching must be a decision from the heart. It must come from a moral imperative to ensure the success of all children and from a commitment to social justice. To be an effective educator today requires far more dedication, talent and commitment than ever before. Anything less is unacceptable. Our students cannot afford to receive anything but the very best from us.

Schools that work for all children have visionary leaders and dedicated and talented teachers who apply the instructional practices that research and experience tell us make a difference. I always aspire to study, seek advice, send staff to workshops, bring in experts and mentors, consult with others and use any other means to increase our staff capacity to make good decisions. All the while I try to continually step into the unknown and encourage staff to do likewise. The risks, however, are calculated to push the boundaries of what is known and commonly done without threatening long-term success.

We must implement multiple teaching approaches to accommodate the multiple learning styles of students and recognize that there are many different kinds of intelligence. Outstanding instructional practices have to become commonplace in all of our schools. Staff development must be fully funded and implemented at all levels. I strongly believe that the only way a school gets better is if the people inside it get better.

Educators have become increasingly aware of the importance of placing high expectations on students' learning. Ron Edmonds and the effective schools research have empirically shown that students will rise to the level of achievement expected of them. A teacher's high expectations for her or his students can be felt by the students. High expectations touch the heart and the head, but too many educators truly don't believe that all children can learn, and that non-belief is communicated, either overtly or subtly, to the students.

In order for educators to believe that all children can learn, many must first unlearn some deeply held societal beliefs. These educators must change their belief that intelligence is fixed at birth, that one's IQ is innate. The common understanding has been that in any population intelligence levels are distributed along a continuum best represented by the bell curve. The bell curve is a mathematical construct designed to illustrate the law of physics that explains the behaviour of random inanimate objects. The use of the bell curve to illustrate intelligence levels has made it legitimate to say that we can't educate all children because not all children are educable. Some educators even rely on tests that are philosophically attached to the bell curve and stipulate that some students will fail, some will succeed and the majority will fall into the middle. The bell curve does not in fact apply to human beings engaged in learning.

When kindergarten children send messages to teachers that indicate they have a lower IQ than expected the response by teachers has generally been lowered expectations. However, if teachers see student potential as developmental, as malleable, as capable of great expansion, then expectations stay high as part of the process of helping students believe in themselves and know that hard work will ensure their success. We must abandon the belief that all the ability that a child will ever have comes at birth. We must believe in the incredible potential to learn that is present in all children and recognize that potential can be realized in any school and in any classroom, if the right conditions exist.

Strong leadership appears in virtually every list characteristics of successful schools. Effective schools research shows us empirically that quality schools require quality principals. In addition, schools need leadership—both formal and informal—that is shared among staff, parents, students and members of the community. Leaders must cultivate a broad definition of community and consider the contributions that every member can make to help our students meet challenging standards. We should hear the voices of many stakeholders, including families, businesses, community organizations and others. Our ability to develop plans that reflect the influence of others is key to our success. Establishing partnerships and listening to a chorus of voices are leadership skills that should permeate all that we do.

Schools must have a purpose, they must have a vision of where they are going. This vision should include a clearly articulated set of core values that serve as the underpinnings for the decisions made on behalf of our students. The school's vision has to be a collective vision, crafted collaboratively. It must be student-centred and focused on ambitious academic goals that are continuously evolving. I believe it is my role to keep the purpose of the school visible, tangible and alive for everyone. I see myself as someone who is dependable and committed, as a "keeper of the dream," who must find real and symbolic ways to keep the mission vital and present on a daily basis in what I write and in my expectations, my words and my daily actions.

Self-assessment is something that I use to demonstrate my accountability to my own values, as well as to the appropriate expectations of our professional community. My preferred approach to self-assessment includes journal keeping, portfolio development, performance indicators and mentors.

It is our experience at Lawrence that students thrive in an environment that provides warmth, love, affection and affirmation. Students do not thrive in an environment where adults are continually critical, constantly accentuating the negative and not accepting children for who they are.

We find that the African proverb that says it takes a whole village to raise a child is especially true today because of the dramatic and alarming changes in our demographics and in our families. This is in contrast to what many of us have been taught in teachers' college. There we were asked to think about "our students" in "our classrooms" almost to the exclusion of the rest of the school. We are often so interested in what happens within our four walls that there is little interest in, or time for, the school as a whole.

It used to be the case at our staff meetings that we would spend more time discussing discipline than curriculum or instruction. During these discussions about discipline the frustrations and confusions caused by challenging student behaviour come out. The discipline at our school has benefited from a philosophy that includes a belief in and practice of firmness, fairness, consistency and positiveness. For all students to feel safe and secure, a clear school-wide policy on discipline must be in place.

An anti-racist and anti-bias curriculum is another part of the daily life at our school. It should be woven into the very fabric of the content of instruction. We must continually seek to be inclusive of diversity in all our teaching. Every child has the right to feel included. This must happen day in and day out, lesson after lesson. Learning is a process not an event, and learning about diversity is most effective when integrated into the daily life of the classroom.

Schools that work for all students must value, appreciate and seek out parental involvement. Many schools experience a low level of parental involvement. Recently we have had success by taking an innovative approach that recognizes we have to get to the students to get to the parents. For us it meant hosting a Playstation tournament for students. For students to participate, their parent had to attend the School Council meeting) and daycare was offered. We have averaged over thirty parents a night. Once we get them here it is our job to keep them coming back. We do this by constantly reminding them that student achievement is clearly linked to parental involvement. We also provide training and seminars that promote the strategic direction of the school.

Student achievement is the key focus of everything we do. We recognize that our students bring different abilities and disabilities into our classrooms. They bring varying degrees of readiness to learn and of parental support to do so. We must continue to hold tenaciously to the view that all students, with no exceptions and no excuses, must be held to high expectations of academic progress, and that skilled and knowledgeable instruction can assist all students.

Recognizing that literacy is the initial key to improving student achievement across the board, we must invest substantial resources in our literacy programs to promote quality literacy instruction in our classrooms. We must, and we will, keep pushing, teaching, cajoling, inspiring our students to read—anything, anywhere, in any language and at any time—because no skill is more vital than reading to a student's success in school and in life.

But teaching our students to read is not enough. We must give them the life, math, science and technology skills they will need to think critically and solve life's problems both in the classroom and out. The good news is that we are doing this, but we can do it even better. We must do it better. This pursuit is and shall remain a journey, not a destination, filled with challenges and, professionally speaking, great rewards. Any success we enjoy is a tribute to our students, staff, parents and community because you, my friends, are simply the best.

Passion and Purpose: A Call for Action

I invite all parents, students, community members, business leaders, school board members, taxpayers and voters to work with us to create the public school system our students and communities deserve: schools that serve as community learning resources and that teach the knowledge and skills needed to prepare students for life.

If you have school aged children:

- get to know your children's teachers
- attend parent–teacher conferences and talk with teachers and your children so that you learn about their needs
- know what kind of assignments teachers expect from your children and make sure your children complete them
- read to preschool children or have older children read to them
- make sure your children see you read regularly
- limit children's television viewing and talking on the phone
- support school efforts to maintain rules for student discipline
- volunteer to support school activities, attend school meetings, join school council
- interest your children in learning outside of school.

If you are a student, demonstrate a love of learning:

- come to school ready to learn, on time
- attend all your classes regularly

- reserve time in your daily schedule for completing homework assignments
- communicate with your teachers, other staff and parents regularly, seeking help from them when you need it
- take advantage of available learning opportunities in and outside of school, during the school year and during times when school is not in session
- read widely: daily newspapers, magazines, library books and books of your own
- be respectful
- set goals
- find a mentor
- be involved at your school.

If you are an employee, support the education program in your community:

- make it easy for parents to attend parent-teacher conferences and other school activities in the school day
- provide opportunities for students and their teachers to visit the workplace or for students to get actual work experience
- require school transcripts and attendance records when hiring young people
- limit the number of hours students work on school nights
- contribute expertise, equipment, or money to help your community's school meet high standards
- participate in the principal-for-a-day program.

If you are an Educator, believe in achieving:

- demonstrate that you care for your students
- make the success of every student your top priority
- set high standards for yourself by continuing to learn and grow throughout your career—be a life long learner
- collaborate with teachers, principals and other colleagues to develop and deliver high quality programs that meet the needs and interests of students
- work with parents and community leaders to develop plans and build support for school improvement efforts
- help students and parents understand why it's important for students to take tough courses
- be part of your school's improvement efforts
- work with others in your school and district to consider how best to use existing resources to help students meet high academic standards
- seek to make your school a family and community learning centre by partnering with local businesses and community organizations to develop before and after school programs for students, adults and families

- be flexible and responsive to the changing needs of students, community and society
- engage students in their own education; rather than being just consumers, they have to be producers
- educate the whole person by developing and implementing a social emotional curriculum
- ensure students learn in an environment which is safe and caring.

Let's put the "public" back in public education:

- involve the public in education by improving access to board meetings
- consider new venues such as libraries, schools, shopping malls or business locations for meetings
- keep up with the education news in your local newspaper
- volunteer to work in your local school as a tutor or mentor
- help give children the right start by supporting social services such as school breakfast and outreach programs
- become a champion for children and education improvement
- evaluate every elected official's track record in support of higher standards and better schools and support those working to improve schools
- don't stop supporting your schools when your children complete their education
- encourage children to use community resources
- attend local school board meetings to inform yourself about what's going on in your schools
- be supportive of innovative and well thought out initiatives.

Afterword

In February 2001 I was promoted to superintendent of schools in the Toronto east education office. The Ministry of Education describes superintendents as officers of the Crown; it is the superintendent who must ensure schools are serving the needs of the students as best they can. Amid all the political goings on in this province we cannot lose sight of this fact.

I became an educator because I felt that I had something to offer students in an educational setting. As an administrator I only expanded the walls of my classroom to include a whole school. My goal has always been the same: to meet the needs of the students. As a superintendent my scope has expanded to include many schools, but I never lose my focus on the students

The need to know myself has become a recurring theme in my leadership development, and having developed emotional intelligence has helped me in my leadership aspirations. It includes knowing what your feelings are and using your feelings to make good decisions in life. It's being able to manage distressing moods well and controlling impulses. It's being motivated and remaining hopeful and optimistic when you have setbacks. It's empathy, knowing what the people around you are feeling. The only way that I can lead, guide, support and contribute to improvement in student outcomes is to know myself.

Leadership is the commitment and capacity to effect change. Few school change efforts are able to succeed without the active involvement of the superintendent. Navigating the turbulent waters of educational reform takes vision and passion. It takes people who place the interests of students before all other interests, who promote workable solutions often in the face of resistance.

One of the many things I learned at Lawrence Heights is that in education, leadership is essential. Leadership matters and does make a difference. Those who desire to lead must commit to a life of service to others. It was Dr. Martin Luther King who said "everyone can be great, because everyone can serve." In truth the accomplishments of leaders are never personal, rather individuals lead when they serve. Effective leadership demands that the greater the authority of the leader, the greater the responsibility of that leader to serve followers.

One person can only do so much. The quality of a leader is almost always determined by the quality of the people he or she can attract. Leadership is not about what you can do, it is about what you can inspire others to do. So how can you tell if you are really serving? It's easy—when your followers begin to thank you more frequently than you have the opportunity to thank them, then you are serving as a leader effectively.

Leadership is also forging a future direction. As a leader, you must establish strategic directions. You must harness change. You must consistently question and seek new answers for changing environments. The late Helen Keller was once asked: What would be worse than to be blind? She replied, "To be born with sight and to have no vision." I firmly believe that you must have a vision. What I suggest is simply laying out the vision and getting everyone moving in the right direction. The right direction is more important than the velocity. Where you are going is more important than how fast you are going to get there. And if you are going to be effective you have to lead by pulling not pushing your staff. Effective leaders must also have the capacity to motivate and empower others to share their sense of direction.

I marvel at the ability of great coaches like Vince Lombardii, Lenny Wilkens or Phil Jackson. Somehow they have the capacity to get everyone of their players to be the best they can be, and move them in the same direction. Leadership inspires others to do great things and you inspire it by your own willingness to work hard. I believe that leaders can't ask

February 15, 2001

To the staff, students and Lawrence Heights community:

We did it.

Faced with a daunting and very public challenge, we got anxious. Then we drew our collective breath and got down to work. And we did it.

We had to. Our neighbours, here and across the province, were watching and we knew it. And before their eyes and before our very own we met the challenge.

Suddenly, each of us had something to prove, some of us were stung by the stigma of having a bad reputation.

We had something to prove, as if we hadn't already proven it time and again, year in and year out, through our role in the countless personal successes of our students, our national award of excellence from the National Quality Institute, our feature article in the Toronto Star and our upcoming feature in Reader's Digest magazine.

But good or bad, fair or unfair, we had to show the world and we had to show ourselves that we were just as good as we knew we were, that we were just as good as we have always been, and that our students were just as able as we have always known them to be.

Some doubted while others believed. But here we are, a year later, and we did it. We've got the results to prove it: our grade 6 students' EQAO scores are up. Now that is something to celebrate.

Finally, I take this opportunity to express my deep sense of gratitude to all of you for making my experience at Lawrence Heights unforgettable. As you have heard, I have been appointed Superintendent of the Borden/Maplewood/West Hill family of schools in Scarborough.

While at Lawrence Heights my bias has been simple: put together the best people, support them and give them every opportunity to do their best work. The best way to reach that goal is equally simple: put together the programs and policies that create a culture of excellence. That ideal has been an essential part of the way we have done business at Lawrence Heights.

Your encouragement, acceptance, support, trust and honesty brought out the "real me" and I could not have asked for a better experience.

Thank you to the most thoughtful, capable, dedicated, knowledgeable and hardworking staff that any principal ever had the privilege of enjoying.

Thank you to the most enthusiastic, talented, spirited and intelligent student body anywhere, and to a community that is rich in diversity, thought and energy.

All of you have been my inspiration and superb guides who have made our journey to excellence at Lawrence Heights remarkable. The journey must continue and I ask you, the Lawrence Heights community, staff and students to be the driving force in ensuring student success.

I thank and honour the staff so very much for your continued professional and personal commitment to our students.

Respectfully yours,

Dr. Christopher Spence

anyone to do anything that they themselves are not willing to do. Leaders lead with integrity. People can see it. I really think that people can peer into a leader's heart, and if there isn't integrity there, they are not going to follow. As you know, there can be no leadership without fellowship. Characteristics alone, of course, do not necessarily make an effective leader. In this regard, leadership is about what you do with who you are, more than just who you are. It's about understanding your strengths and weaknesses, and about taking on leadership roles and responsibilities in which you can connect in an effective way with those who follow you.

Superintendents can bring about change. We can challenge principals and staff to generate ideas for innovation and improvement. We can arrange for and reinforce idea sharing among principals and support their risk taking activities. In order to create a climate where change can flourish, we have to spend time and energy managing issues outside of the schools. This may include being active in a community and public relations. Community members need to understand that our schools are seeking new ways to help students become more successful learners. With their support, change and improvement can be promoted. As a newly-appointed superintendent I am excited about influencing the system, identifying barriers and combating them so that all students can learn. It is what I believe in, what I stand for and what I expect.

Appendix A

School Uniforms

A Needs Assessment

The schools that I visited to discuss school uniform programs stated that the aim of their uniform program was to "establish a calm, businesslike atmosphere at school in which absenteeism would be reduced, school safety would increase and academic performance would rise." One Toronto District School Board school reports that these changes have taken place. They feel that this can largely be attributed to the uniforms and the businesslike atmosphere that has developed.

School uniforms support many of the principles middle school educators are working hard to establish across the province. These educators are trying to develop school environments that nurture adolescents as they struggle to become contributors in our society. Uniforms can help to create an environment in which youth feel comfortable and connected to the school.

During the middle school years, adolescents are busy developing a sense of self. They begin to think about the kind of people they will become. For the students, aged twelve to fourteen, this is a period of lower self-esteem, greater self-consciousness, and a more unstable self-image than experienced by cight- to eleven-year-olds, or adolescents over age fifteen (Steinberg 1989). Students during these years place a greater emphasis on looks, popularity and relationships than in earlier years. Uniforms can help to eliminate one very stressful aspect to this development stage by reducing the need to be fashionable (Steinberg 1989).

Another element of middle school reform that uniforms address is the focus on the whole child. Middle school students can sometimes be cruel. If a child does not have the "right" brand or style of clothing, students can make life very difficult for that child. As one teacher said, "I could always immediately identify my less affluent students by what they were wearing. Some of these students wore the same clothes most every day. Their peers teased them and this was very difficult for these kids. After uniforms, I had a much more difficult time telling which child came from which type of home environment. It really made me think ... was I treating these children based on their socio-economic level? I would certainly hope not, but I cannot be sure." It is important for teachers to help students understand that teasing is not acceptable. Uniforms really help to eliminate this kind of teasing and improve the classroom climate.

Developing a Uniform Program

Administrators who have implemented a uniform program at their schools believe the key to a successful program is parental support. At LH a proposal for school uniforms came directly from our parent council. The whole uniform question is something that everyone has an opinion on. Our staff has had an opportunity to meet parents who, without questions about the uniforms, might not have contacted the school. This initial contact allows conversations about other issues to develop.

In the Lawrence Heights community 93 percent of all parents support the idea of uniforms, but many had questions about the cost. Any initially negative response by parents and others to uniforms usually revolves around the cost of uniforms. What has been demonstrated is that uniforms are generally less expensive than the traditional school clothing purchased at the outset of each year. Eighty percent of parents responding to a uniform program survey in Chicago felt that uniforms represented a more economical way to dress students for school and 84 percent felt that uniforms were easier to maintain than regular dress clothes (Woods and Ogletree 1992).

Students need to be informed of every stage of the plan to develop school uniforms. Although they may not be supportive initially, students find it useful to have opportunities to discuss both sides of the issue. Organizing a student uniform fashion show gives students ownership over and input into the program. This also generates a great deal of interest—at Lawrence Heights more than two hundred parents attended a fashion show—and helps to gain a great deal of acceptance of uniforms. Survey results from incoming grade 5 students reveal 88 percent in favour, while 84 percent of grade 6 and 7 Lawrence Heights students support the idea.

One student from a school with a uniform program told me, "I think the uniform is good because I don't have to worry about what clothes I'm going to wear. At first, I didn't like it, but as the year went on it was better because I didn't have to get up earlier to pick out my clothes. And with everyone else wearing it, it made it easier. Before the uniforms, I was late sometimes because I couldn't decide what to wear. I haven't been late once since the uniform."

I found that the benefits of a uniform program are multifold. While uniforms are not a panacea for violence, they can be an effective part of an overall safety plan created by the entire school community.

Further benefits of school uniforms are:

- The school becomes a place of more serious business and respect
- Uniforms eliminate a source of contention among adolescents
- Uniforms promote school pride
- Uniforms help school officials recognize intruders
- Uniforms simplify the morning routine at home
- Uniforms are inexpensive in comparison to regular clothing.

The information here on the effects of school uniforms is largely anecdotal. School administrators, students and parents have to decide whether uniforms will help reform our schools and improve educational performance. The Lawrence Heights community thinks that they can do this.

The Keys To Staff Success

Lawrence Heights Middle School

As we continue our journey to excellence, please reflect on the following:
Visualize our learning community as one which:
- is compassionate
- values, fosters and supports learning
- provides relevant resources and opportunities
- has a vision and shared goals
- is inclusive.

Visualize our learners as individuals who:
- should assume responsibility for learning
- are lifelong learners
- will have a variety of learning needs
- have needs different from other learners
- need a variety of experiences and opportunities
- should learn independently and with others
- balance working and playing.

Then, to support our learners, our school should be:
- responsive
- adaptable
- respectful of diversity
- empowering
- accessible
- lifelong
- linked to the community.

The Keys:
- Demonstration of care and commitment toward students
- Support for student learning
- Equitable and respectful treatment of students and staff
- Knowledge of students

- High expectations of students
- Knowledge of curriculum
- Knowledge of learning environment
- Effective assessment and evaluation of students
- Evidence of integrated use of technology
- Evidence of planning and preparation
- Evidence of ongoing professional learning
- Extracurricular involvement
- Teamwork
- Ongoing parent communication
- Effective classroom management.

Strategic Plan

We Believe that:
- each child can learn
- each child is important and unique
- there is a direct relationship between expectations and achievement
- everyone has the right to feel safe at school
- integrity and trust are essential to positive interaction
- communication is essential for understanding; understanding is essential for communication
- diversity strengthens the individual, the school and the community
- education is a shared responsibility of the students, parents, educators and the community
- people support, value and respect what they help to create
- planning, both long- and short-term, is essential to achieve student success.

Our Goals

1. To provide all students with a relevant and comprehensive instructional program.
- We will have a continuous process aimed at organizing best educational practices to meet individual student learning needs
- We will continue to improve the design and delivery of instruction
- We will provide programs to develop and evaluate proficiency in listening, speaking, reading, writing, mathematics, science and technology
- We will have students apply knowledge and processes acquired through the study of the arts, sciences, social studies and technology
- We will develop an individual education plan for all students
- We will implement a comprehensive guidance program to prepare students to compete in a global economy

2. To ensure that all students master specified competencies prior to graduation.
- We will report student progress toward meeting individual goals
- We will provide multiple opportunities for student success
- We will train teachers to use a variety of proven assessment methods

3. To meet the individual needs of all students.
- We will provide a wide range of programs to meet the needs of students at all levels of development.
- We will prepare students to work successfully and cooperatively with others and to appreciate diversity
- We will establish and support ethical and caring attitudes
- We will encourage staff to update their skills for a changing population
- We will use existing community programs to avoid duplication of services and to maximize resources

4. To utilize technology to support teaching and learning.
- We will provide hardware and software to support best teaching methods and learning environments (e.g., Learning Equation, Accelerated Reader)
- We will provide technology training for students, staff and parents

5. To provide a safe, orderly and positive environment conducive to teaching and learning.
- We will regularly communicate these expectations
- We will involve staff and community to implement the Toronto District School Board (TDSB) "Safe School" policy and procedures
- We will train staff in safe school initiatives
- We will use successful practices to reduce "at risk" student behaviour
- We will have high expectations for student contact
- We will increase school, community and parent collaborations to promote safe school and community environments

6. To attract and maintain a diverse staff of competent, dedicated caring professionals.
- We will recruit quality staff
- We will expect staff to dress and act professionally
- We will expect staff to follow TDSB policies and procedures
- We will recognize staff for outstanding performance
- We will provide and communicate professional development opportunities to all
- We will provide support services for staff so that they can become more proficient in using technology for effective teaching

7. To promote involvement of all segments of the community as partners in the education of our students.
- We will provide training for parental involvement in education
- We will work effectively with our school council
- We will seek business/community partners for our school
- We will use volunteer resources to support education

8. To communicate effectively.
- We will make regular contact with parents and guardians through phone conversations and the student planner
- We will demonstrate respect and cooperation within a community of individual and cultural differences
- We will establish programs that facilitate two-way communication with our communities
- We will use technology to improve communication
- We will promote our school, its mission, goals, and the successes of its staff and students
- We will produce high-quality and effectively printed materials (newsletter, letters)

9. To responsibly address the financial needs of our school and maximize utilization of resources.
- We will develop alternative revenue sources
- We will develop budgets that show the expenditures needed to accomplish the strategic plan
- We will resolve funding shortages through a prioritization process based on TDSB and school goals

10. To continue strategic planning to achieve our goals.
- We will base decisions on what is best for our children and consistent with TDSB and school goals
- We will establish policies and procedures that support TDSB goals and our mission statement

Appendix C

Eradicating Racism[1]

The eradication of racism is an aim of anti-racist education. Anti-racist education is a pedagogy that advocates critical understanding and concerted action to address the inequity of our society's skewed power structure. It addresses issues of exclusion in our curriculum, of stereotyping in our texts and teaching practices, and of discrimination through all aspects of our institutional and school practices. Anti-racist education emerges from an understanding that racism exists in society and, therefore, the school as an institution of society is influenced by racism.

Anti-racist education attempts to equip teachers and students with the analytical tools to critically examine the origins of racist ideas and practices and to understand the implications of, or struggle against, racism. It provides us with the skills to work collectively to combat racism. It shows the relationship between our personal prejudices and the systematic discrimination that institutions practice on a daily basis. It enables us to see that racism is learned and, therefore, can be unlearned. It exposes the structure in society, and the ways we have organized our lives and institutions to limit some people and advance others on the basis of their race. Anti-racist education moves us beyond the comfortable aspects of each other's cultures, such as food and festivals, so that we can examine the more controversial dimensions of culture which have led to change, and can lead to change.

A stated goal of our multicultural Canadian society is equality of opportunity. Anti-racist education can help us realize that goal by enabling us to analyze the barriers to equal opportunity. It points to structures in our society and relations between the powerful and the powerless which must be changed if we are to achieve true equality of opportunity. Through anti-racist education, we come to understand that it is not because individuals act in bad faith or are inherently unwilling to be accepting of other people, but rather that historical patterns and contemporary situations give us cues as to how we ought to treat each other.

Anti-racist education can teach us how to relate to students' experiences and how to take their needs and problems as the starting point. It can also instruct us to re-educate teachers so that in their classroom practices they may empower students. In the long run this should mean a more democratic and just society can be achieved for everyone.

Key Requirements for the Eradication of Racism from the Classroom

- Continual self-monitoring of reactions, perceptions and attitudes to help overcome our learned racism
- Willingness to develop our own learning about and analysis of social inequities
- Use of all available resources: community members, films, parents and student experiences
- Use of all available allies—community members, parents, students, colleagues, administration, board policies
- Examination and change of selection and organization of material to ensure equity in delivery of curriculum (e.g., identify visible minority people who contributed to the development of knowledge in all subject areas; use visible minority writers to tell their own stories; ensure that the history of all peoples is treated with equal respect)
- Provision of curriculum materials that promote equity through balanced portrayals of all racial groups; continual questioning of assumptions behind one's choice of materials
- Removal of practices in the classroom and the school that emphasize and value mainstream culture over all others (e.g., Christian prayers or reading only, Christian festivals only, white persons on posters and classroom decorations only, "add-on" of token reference to visible minority members, announcement of community events which emphasize mainstream culture only)
- Organization of physical space and working relationships to prevent visible minority students from becoming marginalized (e.g., do not allow these students to remain at the rear of the classroom or at the edges, insist on group work with mixed groups, carefully monitor the roles assigned within groups or in class—do not allow dominant group students to do all the leading or all the validation of student experience)
- Provision of opportunities in all subject areas to introduce issues, questions, assignments, independent study topics, reports, and so forth in which the visible minority student can also be the expert (this might well include the experience of racism)
- Selection of racial minority members from the community to speak with the students on questions other than racism and in other than predictable or stereotyped roles (e.g., on career days, invite a Black lawyer, a South Asian athlete or a Native surgeon; do not invite only a Black athlete or musician)
- Development of alliances and support systems within the school to

provide encouragement and support for students, parents and teachers (e.g., an anti-racist student group needs staff support and a communication network, parent groups need a forum for articulating concerns)

- Encouragement of employment and representational equity in the workplace both by identifying it as an important issue and by pointing out its absence in staffing, on committees and in positions of responsibility
- Identification of equity issues on a regular basis in all classrooms and school activities to assist students to identify and challenge inequity (e.g., questions around the protagonists in the Gulf War, ask why the students have had so few visible minority teachers, question the practice of treating individuals as cultural or racial representatives, ask why there are so few visible minority politicians in Canada)
- Acknowledgment of racism in any and all manifestations when it occurs (clearly state what the issue is using language that leaves no room for interpretation: if it is racism, say so—it IS more than just "bad behaviour")
- Immediate and clear statements of personal reaction to racist occurrences
- Communication of board policy on race relations and clear identification to students and colleagues of anti-racist education as an important and ongoing issue, central to the experience of all students and staff
- Persistence and patience

Outcomes

- An education system in which all students can find a safe place
- An education system in which all students know they are valued
- An education system in which all students are empowered to have their views heard and respected
- An education system in which all students are prepared for full participation in a multiracial, multicultural society
- An education system that provides fair and full opportunity for the development of critical thinking about social issues
- An education system that encourages challenging inequities of power, thus challenging of all inequity
- An education system that will make possible a non-racist society

How Anti-racist are our Schools?

- Does the school have a race relations committee? Does the school have a race relations policy or a similar policy that will meet the needs of this particular school?

- Are students and parents regularly informed of board and school race relations policy?
- Are racist incidents such as name-calling dealt with seriously by the staff and are board personnel regularly consulted about how to deal with such problems and possible solutions?
- Does the material you study include authors from a variety of racial or cultural backgrounds, and do courses stress the contributions of all cultural and racial groups?
- Have you been taught how to detect bias in the materials you teach? Do you have the necessary skills to routinely counteract the bias in the materials studied in the classroom?
- Do the images in school displays, assemblies and community events positively reflect the cultural diversity of students in the school?
- Are the languages other than English spoken by pupils in the school used in displays, notices and announcements?
- Are opportunities provided to ensure that new pupils who are learning English as a second language are welcomed to the school and have an opportunity to work constructively with fluent English speakers?
- Does the food served in the cafeteria reflect the tastes of all racial and ethnic groups?
- Does the school encourage extra-circular activities in which students can explore their cultural heritage and backgrounds?

Note

1. The material is this appendix is adapted from Thomas 1987 and 1985.

A Safe School is a Shared Responsibility

For education to be successful, safe and secure communities and environments must be established. Such environments allow students the opportunity to learn and teachers the opportunity to teach. The mission of the Lawrence Heights safe school committee is to provide leadership in promoting a safe school through collaboration. A safe school is a shared responsibility.

To create havens within which our children can grow and learn, we ask these questions:

- Who is our community?
- How do we involve members of the community?
- What are the needs in our school and community?
- What aspects of the safe school plan do we have in place?
- How can they be improved and better coordinated to work with each other?
- What aspects of the plan are missing?

A school must be a haven for students. In school, students should feel welcomed and comfortable. In order for this to happen all individuals must be valued and respected. Fostering respect for others begins with the attitudes, beliefs and behaviours of the school staff. They must be able to recognize and interpret the biases and directions in their own perceptions and not be quick to assume that students share their view of the world. Teachers must examine their teaching styles and understand that everything they do gives students messages as to their opinion about the students. Education research strongly indicates that positive teacher expectations have a great impact upon students' views of themselves and the world, and ultimately on the quality of their learning.

In creating a climate of respect, schools must encourage the interaction between gender, age, culture and ability groups. As much as possible, schools should reflect the diversity of the Canadian population. Children must have role models who respect diversity. Every staff member must model at all times understanding, acceptance and appreciation of difference.

Students and staff members take pride in their school if students have a sense that they are defining and creating their own environment. They are more willing to take ownership—to feel "this is our world." Programs and/or activities that offer students opportunities to have positive social roles in the school and community have proven successful in increasing the motivation for high-risk students to stay in school and in granting all student participants the satisfaction of positive action.

Students need to be involved in the school at every level. They should serve as members of decision-making teams and as members on other school committees. In addition to inviting students to serve on these committees, schools are encouraged to develop and support opportunities for peer assistance.

Student council can provide students with firsthand experience of democratic processes. Each school should have a duly elected council that has real responsibilities in the workings of the school. Beginning in kindergarten, students need to learn firsthand that with freedom comes responsibility. Student council members will take ownership of the school if they are given the opportunity to participate in discussions centring on ways in which to improve their school. Activities such as school dances and other traditional school events are valuable, but should only be part of the student council agenda. Each student council should, with thoughtful research and discussion, take on some major project and/or activity that will better their school or community.

Peer leadership/mentor programs have also proven valuable both to peer leaders and to their partners. The peer leaders and their advisers receive extensive training in human relations and facilitation skills. They are then matched with younger students, often those who are new to the school. The peer leaders help their partners adjust to the school, promote good study habits, and provide constructive criticism and a concerned ear.

Peer/leadership mentoring can be effective in improving the behaviour and attitudes of both the mentors and those mentored. Mentored students gain needed attention and help that often a teacher does not have the time to provide. They also have before them influential role models who demonstrate the positive side of academic and behavioural success. Mentors gain a sense of satisfaction and pride in helping someone else. All also gain interpersonal skills and a sense of pride in themselves and their school.

A safe schools plan must include a community supported effort to see that students can confidently travel to and from school through "safe" neighbourhoods where residents are constantly looking out for their protection.

The school's code of behaviour needs to be developed and supported by students, staff and the community. In clear concise language, the code must establish and emphasize ethical commonality comprising core values such as honesty and respect for others. It must include the rights and responsibilities of both adults and students within the school community. It is important to set out explicitly the responsibilities of all members of the school community in order to make it clear that everyone in the school is held to the same standards. These responsibilities must become an active focus within the school and community. Students as well as adults must feel ownership for the code of behaviour.

The Lawrence Heights safe school committee had the following goals for the 1998/1999 school year:

The School's Physical Environment

Goal: To provide an environment where students, staff, parents and community feel a sense of self, school and community pride, and a commitment to creating a safe and nurturing climate at Lawrence Heights Middle School.

Objectives: Continue progress in beautifying the school, and develop and implement a recognition process for students, staff and community that highlights their contributions to the school environment.

School Social Environment

Goal: To strengthen the sense of commitment of students, parents, administration, staff and the community to creating a positive and supportive environment at Lawrence Heights Middle School and in the neighbourhood.

Objectives: School rules will be communicated to and understood by all students, staff and parents. Violations will be dealt with in a fair and consistent manner; Lawrence Heights staff and parents will be offered opportunities to express their opinions and take part in decision making regarding school policies and procedures; and Lawrence Heights staff will strive to decrease the number of classroom disruptions, provide cooperative learning experiences for students at all ability levels and insure that all students have a positive self-concept.

June 2001
Reader's Digest

"Believe You Can"

This Toronto school had a bad reputation. And it was just the challenge Chris Spence was looking for.

By Margo Pfeiff

On his first tour of Lawrence Heights Middle School (LHMS), Chris Spence was led past defaced bulletin boards in hallways scribbled with graffiti. Peering into the library, he saw kids with their feet on the tables, competing to see who could throw books the farthest out the window. It was June 1997 and Lawrence Heights was looking for a new vice principal. The 35-year-old spoke with some of the staff, like classroom assistant Claire Davis, who told of student rampages in which desks were overturned and chairs thrown about. Police had been called in to break up fights. Two boys had recently been suspended for "mooning" their female teacher in class. More than half the teachers transferred annually.

But Spence eagerly took the job; Lawrence Heights was exactly what he was looking for. To announce the new vice principal's appointment, an assembly was called; it was cut short when a fight erupted.

Just north of downtown Toronto, the Lawrence Heights area comprises mostly public-housing complexes. At LHMS, which offers Grades 6, 7 and 8, 87 percent of the students or their parents are immigrants from some 31 countries; 24 languages are spoken in the hallways. Drug dealers, gangs and the sound of gunfire weren't uncommon in the neighbourhood. Parents who could sent their children to schools elsewhere.

During his first year at LHMS, Spence spent most of his time on discipline rather than the issues he considered paramount: abysmal grades and low attendance. LHMS excelled at only one thing: sports. The school was renowned for its outstanding teams, especially basketball. Many boys dreamed of reaching the NBA.

Spence understood that dream well. Born in England, Spence emigrated with his family to Canada when he was seven. Football was Spence's dream, and he lived it when the B.C. Lions drafted the tall, stocky running back in 1985. But a torn Achilles tendon ended his career after just two seasons, and he realized that focusing only on sports had limited his education. He vowed to help other youngsters avoid that trap. Inspired, he earned a master's and then a doctorate in education.

When he graduated in 1991, he could have chosen any Toronto school, but he chose Oakdale, in a largely immigrant neighbourhood where violence was common. For many students, he was their first Black teacher. "It's where I can make a difference," he told his colleagues. Six years later, driven by his desire to reach more children, he set his sights on taking the helm of a school.

Dress for Success

In May 1998, the end of Spence's first year as LHMS vice principal, the principal was transferred and Spence took over. He immediately called the teachers together. "We're going to make every student and teacher proud of Lawrence Heights," he told them, "but I need your ideas." He was greeted with enthusiasm. "How about letting my students paint murals on the walls and lockers during the summer?" art teacher Zelia Tavares suggested. "Great idea," Spence replied. "We'll let the kids choose the designs."

That summer, as youngsters transformed the school with multicultural murals and positive slogans, Spence laid plans. In early September he called an assembly. The restless crowd, topped in cornrows, blond curls and Muslim scarves, already admired Spence as a sports hero, but they were not prepared for his authoritarian tone. "You will sit and listen," he began in his no-nonsense voice. "The atmosphere at this school is not conducive to learning. There is too much fear and intimidation. For a start, I will not tolerate fighting." Extracurricular activities like sports, clubs and dances would become privileges — and they would be withdrawn for bad behaviour.

"Why do we honour our basketball and football teams," he asked, pointing to the championship banners hanging above their heads, "but have not a word of praise for students who do well academically?" At the "new" LHMS, top students would receive medals at monthly assemblies, and Academic All Stars would be celebrated in a rally, "just as we cheer our athletes."

Spence bombarded the 290 students with the reality of their performance: scores below city and provincial averages in math, reading and writing; one of the worst reputations for violence; and hundreds of suspensions and more than 3,000 "lates" registered the previous year. "In the real world, lateness is a prime reason for being fired," he explained, "so most of you couldn't even hold a job." School would now *be* their job. "Each student will sign a contract vowing to be on time, do their homework and be respectful.

"This can be a great school," he continued. "Let's work together."

S pence put uniforms on the agenda for the year's first parent-teacher meeting. "Competition between children who can afford the latest fashions and those who can't is unhealthy," Spence said. "I'm suggesting white shirts and black bottoms of your choosing, and a school pin." The parents voted 96 percent in favour. Now he had to convince the children. "I've seen students beaten up because they can't afford high fashion," he told each grade. "Is that fair?" The students, too, voted "yes" to Dress for Success.

Over 70 percent of the area's families were single-parent homes; many children returned each day to empty houses. So Spence encouraged teachers to create appealing extracurricular activities. Soon the hallways echoed with Hindi music as sari-clad girls of Indian descent practised traditional dance, while others learned African drumming for the annual Cultural Showcases.

When Charmaine Marine, a former music specialist at LHMS, visited, Spence urged her to revive the choir she'd started during her tenure there. Marine agreed. Like Spence, she demanded perfection. "So you want to be a star?" she barked to more than 100 students at the first practice. "Then be on time or don't waste my time." They came on time, and even early, for 7:30 a.m. practices and for Saturday sessions.

Silence the Violence

Ending violence remained Spence's first mission. He designated separate stairways for Grades 6 and 7 to keep the older children from picking on younger ones. He singled out students who caused problems and spent time with them. "My door is always open," he told them. One of the most disruptive was 11-year-old Jimoy Rae, a verbally abusive, angry young man who continually fought with others.

S pence saw intelligence and potential in the young man. He visited Jimoy's home to meet his mother, Noele Taylor, who was raising Jimoy and four siblings alone. Spence encouraged Jimoy, took an interest in his schoolwork and placed him in a counselling and support group for troubled, at-risk youths. Soon Jimoy began waiting patiently outside Spence's office after school to talk. Within months he was regularly volunteering to help out in the office.

When Taylor heard Spence's voice on the phone one afternoon, she was filled with fear. Then she heard the principal tell her he had just watched Jimoy walk away from a fight saying, "I don't have time for that anymore." She was flooded with relief. "I've never had a call from school with good news," she said, her voice trembling. At the end of Grade 7, Jimoy Rae stood proudly at the front of the assembled school to receive a medal for the student with the best academic improvement for the year.

Spence acted swiftly at the first sign of a confrontation. He immediately suspended the students involved from sports and extracurricular activities. But most effective were the Friday assemblies called Name and Shame but nicknamed by students the Good, Bad and Ugly. They started on a positive note. "Give yourselves a hand," Spence would say after announcing the week's achievements. But then he would single out anyone involved in brawls or encounters with the law. Fights became rare.

Spence also rewarded good behaviour. School dances became monthly events. Fund-raising and improved grades brought free trips to Raptors and Argos games or to the hottest concerts in town.

King of Mottoes

"Good morning, Lawrence Heights," Spence broadcast over the PA system each morning, and at day's end he signed off with a positive slogan. The principal became affectionately known as the King of Mottoes, and the youngsters picked them up like rap mantras. "The more you learn, the more you earn" was a favourite. "Believe you can achieve," the school's catchphrase, was emblazoned across lockers.

Spence and Vice Principal Tracy Hayhurst stood in the hallway amid a flow of black-and-white uniforms between classes. Spence ate his lunch surrounded by students in the cafeteria and seemed to know everyone by name. "In most schools you need binoculars to find the principal," Greater Toronto School Board community advisor Lawrence George commented during a visit.

As distrust between teachers and students dissolved, students reported misbehaviour: Once, an intruder bent on theft was apprehended after a student noticed his street clothes. The atmosphere became lively and relaxed: Boys greeted Spence with high fives; girls linked arms with him to chat about his baby daughter.

By Christmas 1999, suspensions and lates had plummeted, but there was little improvement in report-card marks. Over the holidays Spence devised a plan, and in January he called the parents together.

"We'd like to monitor students with a monthly report," he told them. Teachers would judge performance and note whether homework was done. Falling back in any subject, missing a day of school, arriving late for class or dressing sloppily would mean an instant suspension from extracurricular activities until the next report. The parents were in favour and had only one suggestion: "Can you make it every two weeks?" Taken aback by their fervour, Spence agreed.

Moans and complaints echoed throughout the gym when progress reports were introduced during assembly. Spence held up LHMS's interscholastic math scores. "We beat this school by 40 points in basketball, and they beat us by the same score in math," he told them. "Who's going to be whose boss?" Spence paused. "I'm not asking you to be straight-A students. I'm trying to make it possible for you to get into the high school or university of your choice." The students voted "yes" to progress reports.

Every second Friday, when progress reports were posted for all to see, the hallways were the scene of crying and whoops of joy. Students had to pass Spence and Hayhurst as they headed home. "What happened here?" Spence would sometimes ask. Then parents had to be faced, as their signatures were required on the reports. The bulletin board outside the office became a barometer of the school's progress.

"If you get a No, you can't go" became the new slogan, and the fallout hit quickly. When Marine arrived one Saturday to take her choir to a TV performance, only 14 students were on the bus. "What's going on?" she demanded of those standing alongside. "We got No's," they sobbed. They never did again.

A week before the Grade 8 boys' district basketball championship game, the two top players received No's. LHMS lost. "You let our school down, man," heartbroken students told the suspended players. Neither received a No again.

"Words Aren't Enough"

When school resumed in September 1999, Spence's second year, the principal received a call. Karlene Thompson explained that her son Donohue Grant, 13, was constantly in trouble. He attended another school but didn't like it and was now charged with assault. "I don't know what to do," said Thompson.

In Donohue, Spence and teacher Tim Skinner found a troubled but very bright young man and a gifted athlete. Both accompanied him to court, vowing on the stand to remain involved in his education and care. Spence gave Donohue a Grade 7 crash course to make up for time lost during previous suspensions and sometimes took him home for dinner with his family. Donohue blossomed with the attention.

One winter day Spence arrived at school to find Donohue helping the custodian shovel snow. Soon the young man began counselling children and helping coach basketball. When his mother noticed him doing more studying than shooting baskets and commented on it, he said, "There's plenty of time for ball. I've got to get a career." Donohue, found innocent of the assault charges, stood up before the entire school at the end of the year to receive the annual leadership award for helping others. The following day he and his mother appeared at Spence's office. "Words alone aren't enough to thank you," Thompson said as Donohue handed Spence a plaque. "A Certificate of Appreciation," he read through a mist of tears. "Thanks for everything."

A Model School

To prepare for provincial reading, writing and math exams in April 2000, students voted to suspend all extracurricular activities. The result? Lawrence Heights rated above not only the Toronto average but the provincial average as well. Last fall LHMS became the only school that year to receive the Canada Award for Excellence from the National Quality Institute, which honours an organization's commitment to excellence and superior standards.

In just three years Spence has created what would be a model school in any part of Canada. At the end of the 1999-2000 school year, there had been only a handful of fights and lates had dropped to 400. There's a waiting list to teach at LHMS. Says Denise Earle, Parent Council chairman and mother of three LHMS children, parents have noticed a big change in their children. "They have more control of their feelings," she says. "They are more respectful."

"What we're doing is not rocket science," Spence says with a shrug. "We're just creating a positive learning environment that puts the emphasis back on academics." Sports can be a valuable tool, he believes. "But you still need another career. And that starts in the classroom."

Game plan

Lawrence Heights students thrive under former CFL running back's 'winning' academic vision

By Kristin Rushowy, Education Reporter

Want to play on the school basketball team? Sing in the choir? Be in the photography club?

Then know the drill: Don't be late. Wear your uniform. Come prepared.

Every day, no excuses.

This is life for the Grades 6, 7 and 8 students at Lawrence Heights Middle School—a daily regimen where you play by the rules. What else to expect when your principal is a former Canadian Football League player?

Chris Spence is big on discipline and he can be tough. But being a part of his team means if you get things done, and done well, you'll feel like a winner.

"He does unbelievable stuff for us," says Grade 8 student Nathaniel Mitchell, 13, who considers Spence "like a second dad."

"He's like a best friend," adds 12-year-old Venus Sayed, also in Grade 8. "You can drop in and see him any time, and talk about anything."

Spence, a running back, played for the B.C. Lions in 1985 and 1986, but was out for the '87 season because of an Achilles tendon injury. In 1988, while playing for Winnipeg, he realized the injury was too serious for him to continue.

He turned to education to turn his life around, getting a bachelor's degree in education at York University, then a master's and Ph.D. at the University of Toronto.

He arrived at Lawrence Heights three years ago with a vision.

"One of the things I wanted to initiate was coming up with something on paper that we'd strive for each and every day when we came in. We were striving for excellence in all that we do," explains Spence, 37.

"The only thing we are asking is that you be a better student today than you were yesterday."

That vision reaches into every corner of Lawrence Heights, a diverse school where 87 per cent of students, or their parents, are immigrants. Spence and his vice-principal Tracy Hayhurst have weekly meetings - pep talks - with students.

Spence is also big on slogans. Some are painted on the walls and lockers: "Believe you can achieve" has become the school's catchphrase.

"I'm king of the mottoes," he laughs. "We get on the P.A. every day and we start with a motto, every morning.

"Everywhere they go in this school, we want there to be some reminder. When you walk out the door, there's a sign we hope they internalize and take when they walk out, and that's 'learning is for life.'"

To get kids interested in academics, Spence and his staff use the "dangle the carrot" philosophy.

Last year, they started doing monthly progress reports, in which teachers fill out a form for each student, checking off "yes" or "no" in categories such as arriving on time, homework completion or dressing for success (wearing uniforms). Students take the form home and must return it after their parents sign it.

Spence has no reservations about not allowing students to take part in after-school activities, watch sporting events or even pulling players off teams if they get even one no.

"It's right there, and they know it," he says. "Any event, I'm standing at that door and they have to show it (their progress report) to me before they can get in.

"The only way you can do that is to have lots of opportunities at the school."

It doesn't mean students have to get all A's, but they have to focus on school and behave well. Because the reports are done regularly, students can get back on teams within a month if they pull themselves up.

The idea was a bit controversial and "it hurt our choir, it hurt our teams," Spence admits.

But the payoffs? Unbelievable. Teachers say there is a real focus on studies at the school. And why not? Students are rewarded by taking part in the athletics teams and other non-academic extracurricular activities, such as the pet or photography club. They can use the school's new games room.

Spence even takes two students from each grade to Argos or Raptors games on occasion and great concerts, like Puff Daddy or Boyz II Men. Money from fundraisers pays for the tickets.

Choristers get to go on out-of-town trips. Those who went to Windsor last year got a special treat.

"(Spence) took us all to his parents' house for lunch," says Raymond Lieu, 12.

Last month, only students who had completed a summer homework package were allowed to try out for YTV's UH OH! game show when it came to the school.

"You meet them halfway," says Spence. "You want to give them evidence of the things we are willing to do, things to make them want to learn.

"I'm convinced the kids we have in this school want to learn; they want to be at school. It didn't just happen. It took a concerted effort and vision as to where we wanted to go.

"As educators now, we have to find innovative ways, do things differently, all to reach the same end."

Teachers, and students, have noticed the difference.

Sandra Webster, a Grade 6 teacher who's been at the school for four years, says children's self-esteem has grown tremendously.

"There is a spark, a positive energy. Even for us teachers, we are part of a team, with the same vision."

She says the progress reports and uniforms have made the biggest impact.

"Everything is monitored and tracked; students earn extracurricular activities. All of these things make kids more accountable for their actions and they focus more on goal-setting."

"We're always told that education comes first, that we always have to get our work done," says Emma Jeddi, 12, who's in Grade 7.

"Academics is above anything else," adds Venus. "I think it's good; they try and persuade students to do their work, and for those who aren't interested in school, it gets them working because they want to take part in the activities. The activities we get here are great."

One is the pet friend club, where students help look after animals at the school including Marvin the ferret.

Grade 6 student Bethlehem Kifle, 11, came from a junior school where students didn't wear uniforms. Now she thinks they're great.

"They give us more discipline. We realize that we come here to learn."

For students who do achieve high grades, they share in the glory of Lawrence Heights' "Academic All-Stars."

Staff saw the kind of spirit students had for sports and they wanted to translate that to academics, says Spence.

So, once a month, the top 10 students from each grade are treated like athletes returning home triumphant from the big game.

"Now, those kids sitting in the assembly see their peers going up there and getting a medal, and they want to be up there. They love that kind of stuff.

"In the past, the only time we ever did that was for sport. The basketball team would win the championship and come back and we'd play the music and everybody would feel so great about it.

"We said, 'Geez, if we could get the same for academics' ... because that's the ticket for them. That's what's going to get them into the university they want to go to, the job they want to get."

Grade 6 teacher Ed Malabre, who is also head of math, science and technology at the school, says students find Spence, and the atmosphere at the school, inspiring.

"His energy, his enthusiasm, his fairness and, the most important thing, his dedication and commitment to take the good, the bad and the ugly and give the students here at Lawrence Heights an advantage."

Spence isn't the first football-player-turned-principal. He follows in the footsteps of Russ Jackson, a CFL hall-of-famer.

He believes a lot of the skills football players learn are life skills - discipline, dedication, being a team player.

"From the day I was born, I heard my parents tell me how important education is," Spence says.

"My first love, my first career was football. When that opportunity no longer existed, education became my football. All my life's ambitions, my hard work was part of being the best educator I could. I really wanted to make a meaningful impact on as many kids as I could.

"No matter what sport it is, it's fleeting at best. You're always going to need a second career, and you need to get yourself in a position to do those things. It all starts in the classroom."

Reprinted with permission—The Toronto Star Syndicate.

Bibliography

Archbald, D.A., and F.M. Newmann. 1988. *Beyond Standardized Testing: Assessing Authentic Academic Achievement in the Secondary School.* Reston,VA: National Association of Secondary School Principals.

Bates, P. 1990. "Desegregation: Can We Get There From Here." *Educational Leadership* 72,1.

Bennett, Barrie, Carol Rolheiser-Bennett and Laurie Stevahn. 1991. *Co-Operative Learning: Where Heart Meets Mind.* Toronto: Educational Connections.

Bernard, B. 1991. *Fostering Resiliency in Kids: Protective Factors in the Family, School, and Community.* Portland: Northwest Regional Educational Laboratory.

Best, John. 1987. "Equity in Education?" *Kappa Delta Pi Record* XXIII.

Children's Express. 1993. *Voices From the Future: Children Tell us about Violence in America.* New York: Crown.

Clark, B. 1979. *Growing Up Gifted: Course Lectures and Readings.* Columbus, OH: Charles Merrill.

_____ 1992. *Growing Up Gifted.* 4th Edition. Columbus, OH: Charles Merrill.

Cochrane, O., D. Cochrane, S. Scalena and E Buchanan. 1984. *Reading, Writing, and Caring.* Winnipeg: Whole Language Consultants.

Coelho, Elizabeth. 1988. *Co-Operative Learning and Language Acquisition.* North York: North York Schools.

_____. 1988. *Co-Operative Learning and Academic Achievement.* North York: North York Schools.

_____. 1988. *Co-Operative Learning and Race Relations.* North York: North York Schools.

Coleman, J.B., and T. Hoffer. 1987. *Public and Private High Schools: The Impact of Communities.* New York: Basic Books.

Collins, Marva. 1992. *Ordinary Children, Extraordinary Teachers.* Charlottesville, VA: HamptonBroad Publishing.

Coloroso. B. 1987. *Discipline: Winning at Teaching.* Littleton, CO: Kids Are Worth It.

Delpit, L. 1996. "The Politics of Teaching Literate Discourse." In W. Ayers and P. Ford (eds.), *City Kids, City Teachers: Reports From the Front Row.* New York: New York Press.

Denbo, Sheryl. 1997. *Improving Schools for Language Minority Children.* Washington: National Academy Press.

Diderat, Seenis. 1953. *Diderat: Selected Philosophical Writings.* John Lough (ed.). Cambridge: Cambridge University Press.

Dreikurs, R., B. Grunwalk and F. Peper. 1982. *Maintaining Sanity in the Classroom: Classroom Management Techniques.* New York: Harper and Row.

Drucker, Peter. 1997. *Managing the Future.* New York: Jossey-Bass.

Edmonds, R.R. 1977. *Search for Effective Schools: The Identification and Analysis of City Schools that are Instructionally Effective for Poor Children.* (ED 142 610). Boston MA: Harvard University.

_____. 1979a. "Effective Schools for the Urban Poor." *Educational Leadership* 37.

_____. 1979b. "Some Schools Work and More Can." *Social Policy* 9,5.

Eccles, J. 1987. *Understanding Motivation: Achievement Beliefs, Gender Roles and Changing Educational Environments.* New York: Academic Press.

Ennis, Robert H. 1976. "Equality of Educational Opportunity." *Educational Theory* 26, 1.

Fullan, M., and A. Hargreaves. 1998. *What's Worth Fighting For Out There?* Toronto: Ontario Public School Teachers' Federation

Gardner, H. In press. "Assessment in Context: The Alternative to Standardized Testing." In B. Gifford and M.C. O'Conner (eds.), *Future Assessments: Changing Views of Aptitude, Achievement, and Instruction.* Boston: Kluwer Academic Publishers.

Gibbs, Jeanne. 1998. *Guiding Your School Community to Live a Culture of Caring and Learning.* San Clemente, CA: Kagan Publishers.

Goleman, D. 1997. *Emotional Intelligence.* NY: Bantam.

Green, S.J.D. 1988. "Is Equality of Opportunity a False Idea for Society?" *British Journal of Sociology* 39, 1.

Gursky, D. 1990. "The Greatest Challenge: A Plan that Works." *Teacher* 1,9.

Halkitis, P. 1988. "Grouping of 3 in the Science Classroom." *The Gifted Child Today* 11, 5.

Hargreaves, Andy. 1997. ASCD *Year Book: Rethinking Educational Change with Heart and Mind.* Alexandria, VA: ASCD

_____. 1997. "Rethinking Educational Change: Going Deeper and Wider in the Quest for Success." In Hargreaves 1997: 216–33.

Hawkins, C. 1994. *Understanding Adolescents: An IPPF Report on Young Peoples' Sexual and Reproductive Needs.* London: International Planned Parenthood Federation.

Higgins, G. 1994. *Resilient Adults: Overcoming a Cruel Past.* San Francisco: Jossey-Bass.

Hodgkinson, Harold L. 1985. *All One System: Demographics of Education, Kindergarten Through Graduate School.* Washington: Institute for Educational Leadership.

Johnson, D., R.T. Johnson and E.J. Holubec. 1990. *Cooperation in the Classroom.* Revised edition. Edina, MN: Interaction Book Company.

Knapp, M.S., B.J. Turnbull, and P.M. Shields. 1990. "New Directions for Educating Children of Poverty." *Educational Leadership* 48,1.

Knapp, M.S., and Associates. 1995. *Teaching for Meaning in High Poverty Classrooms.* New York: Teachers College.

Kohn, A. 1993. "Choices For Children: Why and How to Let Students Decide." *Phi Delta Kappan* 75, 1 (September).

Labinowicz, E. 1980. *The Piaget Primer: Thinking, Learning—Teaching.* Menlo Park, CA: Addison-Wesley.

Letgers, N., E. McDill and J. McPartland. 1993. "Section II Rising to the Challenge:

Emerging Strategies for Educating Students at Risk." In Rossi 1993: 49–92).

Levine, D.U., and L.W. Lezotte. 1990. *Unusually Effective Schools: A Review and Analysis of Research and Practice*. Madison: The National Centre for Effective Schools Research and Development.

Lifton, R. 1994. *The Protean Self: Human Resilience in an Age of Fragmentation*. New York: Basic Books.

Lomotey, K. 1989. "Cultural Diversity in the School: Implications for Principals." *NASSP Bulletin* 73, 521.

Malcolm, S. 1988. "Brilliant Women for Science, Mathematics, Engineering. Getting More Than We Deserve?" Paper presented at Duke University, Durham, N.C.

McDill, Edward L., Gary Natriello and Aaron M. Pallas. 1986. "Raising Standards and Retaining Students: The Impact of the Reform Recommendations on Potential Dropouts." *Review of Educational Research* 55,4 (Winter).

McIntosh, Peggy. 1988. "White Privilege and Male Privilege: A Personal Account of Coming to See Correspondence through Work in Women's Studies." Wellesley College Centre for Research on Women Working Paper No. 189.

Meier, D. 1995. *The Power of Their Ideas: Lessons for America From a Small School in Harlem*. Boston: Beacon Press.

Moles, O.C. 1992. "Synthesis of Recent Research on Parent Participation in Children's Education." *Educational Leadership* 40, 2.

Natriello, G., E.L. McDill, and A.M. Pallas. 1990. *Schooling Disadvantaged Children: Racing Against Catastrophe*. New York: Teachers College.

Northwest Regional Educational Laboratory. 1990. *School Improvement Research Series*. Portland, OR: US Department of Education.

O'Brien, Dick. 2000. "Never a Bad Day." Keynote address, Lawrence Heights Middle School. April 25.

Ontario Ministry of Education. 1975. *The Formative Years*. Ottawa: Ontario Ministry of Education.

_____. 1985. *Programming for the Gifted*. Ottawa: Ontario Ministry of Education.

_____. 1986. *Discipline Resource Guide*. Ottawa: Ontario Ministry of Education.

_____. 1988. *Behaviour Resource Guide*. Ottawa: Ontario Ministry of Education.

Popkewitz, T.S., and S. Myrdal. 1991. *Case Studies of the Urban Mathematics Collaborative Project: A Report to the Ford foundation*. Madison: University of Wisconsin-Madison, School of Education, Wisconsin, Wisconsin Centre for Education Research.

Revicki, D.A. 1991. *The Relationship Among Socio-economic Status, Home Environment, Parent Involvement, Child Self-Concept, and Child Achievement*. (ED 206 645). Chapel Hill, NC: University of North Carolina.

Rossi, R.J. (ed.). 1993. *Schools and Students at Risk: Context and Frameworks for Positive Change*. New York: Teachers College Press.

Royal Commission of Learning. 1994. "Equity Considerations." *For the Love of Learning*. Toronto: Queen's Printer of Ontario.

Rutter, M. 1984. "Resilient Children." *Psychology Today* March.

_____. 1985. "Family and School Influences on Cognitive Development." *Journal of Child Psychology and Psychiatry* 26.

Rutter, M., B. Maughan, P. Mortimore, J. Ouston and A. Smith. 1979. *Fifteen Thousand Hours*. Cambridge: Harvard University.

Sadker, M., and D. Sadker. 1985. "A Model Program for Gifted Girls in Science."

Journal for the Education of the Gifted XII, 2.

Scharr, John H. 1967. "Equality of Opportunity and Beyond." In A. de Crespigny and A. Wertheimer (eds.), *Contemporary Political Theory.* London: Nelson.

School Improvement Program. 1990. *Effective Schooling Practices: A Research Synthesis.* Portland: Northwest Regional Educational Laboratory.

Seligman, M. 1995. *The Optimistic Child.* Boston: Houghton Mifflin.

Short, Thomas. 1988. "Diversity and Breaking the Disciplines. Two New Assaults on the Curriculum." *Academic Questions* 1, 3 (Summer).

Soder, R., and R. Andrews. 1985. "Equity and Excellence: The Moral Imperatives of Compulsory Schooling." *Curriculum in Context* 6, 9.

Spence, C. 1999. *The Skin I'm In.* Halifax: Fernwood.

_____. 1996. *Teammates the Film.* Brampton, ON: CMS Productions.

Steele, C.M. 1992. "Race and Schooling of Black Americans." *Atlantic Monthly* 26,4.

Steinberg, L. 1989. *Adolescence.* 2nd edition. New York: McGraw Hill.

Thomas, B. 1987. "Anti-Racist Education: A Response to Manicom." In J. Yound (ed.). *Breaking the Mosaic: Ethnic Identities in Canadian Schooling.* Toronto: Garamond.

_____. 1985. "Principles of Anti-Racist Education." *Currents* 3,2.

Toronto Board of Education. 1980. *Observing Children.* Toronto: Toronto Board of Education.

United States Department of Education. 1990. National Forum on Personnel Needs for Districts with Changing Demographics: Staffing the Munti-Cultural Schools in the 1990's. Washington: United States Department of Education, Office of Multi-Cultural Education.

Walberg, Herbert J., Rosanne A. Paschal and Thomas Weinstein. 1985. "Homework's Powerful Effects on Learning." *Educational Leadership* 42, 7.

Wehlage, Gary G., and Robert A. Rutter. 1986. "Evaluation of Model Program for At Risk Students." Paper presented at the annual meeting of the American Educational Research Association, San Francisco.

Wells, Hon. Thomas L. 1976. *Education in the Primary and Junior Division.* Ottawa: Ontario Ministry of Education.

Werner, E. 1996. "How Kids Become Resilient: Observations and Cautions." *Resiliency in Action* 1, 1.

Werner, E., and R. Smith. 1992. *Overcoming the Odds: High Risk Children From Birth to Adulthood.* New York: Cornell University.

Williams, John H. 1993. "What Makes A Great Student? Clarifying Grade Expectations." *The Teaching Professor* 7,7. Pepperdine University.

Woods, H., and E. Ogletree. 1992. "Parents' Opinions of the Uniform Student Dress Code." ERIC Document Service No. ED 367729.

Also by Chris Spence

The Skin I'm In
Racism, Sports and Education

Christopher M. Spence

Fernwood Publishing
ISBN 1 55266 017 6 $15.95

This book discusses the role that sport participation plays in the lives of Black male high-school students. As a former professional athlete himself, the author brings a firsthand, personal quality to this study. As an educator he strives to counteract the problems associated with students who place sport participation ahead of academic achievement. Dr. Spence also seeks to educate educators to fight against inequality and racism in mainstream education and all of us to fight injustices in society.

"We have raped a generation of young black athletes. We have taken kids and sold them on bouncing a ball and running with a football and that being able to do certain things athletically was an end in itself. We cannot afford to do that to another generation."—Joe Paterno, Head Football Coach, Penn State Univ.

Made in the USA
Lexington, KY
12 December 2014